GARDENING WITH
SCENTED PLANTS

GARDENING WITH
SCENTED PLANTS

TONY HALL

Kew Publishing
Royal Botanic Gardens, Kew

Royal Botanic Gardens Kew

© The Board of Trustees of the Royal Botanic Gardens, Kew 2025

Photographs © Tony Hall unless otherwise stated

The author has asserted their rights as author of this work in accordance with the Copyright, Designs and Patents Act 1988.

All rights reserved. No part of this publication may be reproduced, stored in a retrieval system, or transmitted, in any form, or by any means, electronic, mechanical, photocopying, recording or otherwise, without written permission of the publisher unless in accordance with the provisions of the Copyright Designs and Patents Act 1988.

Great care has been taken to maintain the accuracy of the information contained in this work. However, neither the publisher, the editors nor author can be held responsible for any consequences arising from use of the information contained herein. The views expressed in this work are those of the author and do not necessarily reflect those of the publisher or of the Board of Trustees of the Royal Botanic Gardens, Kew.

First published in 2025 by
Royal Botanic Gardens, Kew,
Richmond, Surrey, TW9 3AB, UK
www.kew.org

ISBN 978 1 84246 836 4

Distributed on behalf of the Royal Botanic Gardens, Kew in North America by the University of Chicago Press, 1427 East 60th St, Chicago, IL 60637, USA.

British Library Cataloguing in Publication Data
A catalogue record for this book is available from the British Library

Design: Kevin Knight
Page layout: Christine Beard
Project management: Georgina Hills
Copy-editing: James Kingsland
Proofreading: Sharon Whitehead

Printed and bound in Italy by L.E.G.O. S.p.A

EU Authorised Representative: Easy Access System Europe Oü, 16879218. Mustamäe tee 50, 10621, Tallinn, Estonia (email: gpsr.requests@easproject.com).

For information or to purchase all Kew titles please visit shop.kew.org/kewbooksonline or email publishing@kew.org

Kew's mission is to understand and protect plants and fungi, for the wellbeing of people and the future of all life on Earth.

Kew receives approximately one third of its funding from Government through the Department for Environment, Food and Rural Affairs (Defra). All other funding needed to support Kew's vital work comes from members, foundations, donors and commercial activities, including book sales.

LEFT
Wall-trained *Wisteria sinensis*

Contents

Introduction	6
Scent	10
Herbs	12
Scent and wildlife	14
Annuals and biennials	18
Bulbs	26
Climbers	40
Herbs	54
Perennials	68
Shrubs	80
Trees	122
Glossary	140
Further reading	141
Flowering by month	142
Flower colours	156
Plants with scented foliage	166
Plants for wildlife	167
Index	169

ABOVE
Honey-scented *Spartium junceum*

Introduction

There was a time when many garden plants were grown not only for their colour and form but also for their complex and attractive scents. This was particularly true in the cottage-style garden, where roses and scented perennials were a large part of the overall scheme. In fact, humans have valued scented garden plants for thousands of years.

Paintings and frescoes from Ancient Egypt show priests growing fragrant plants in their walled gardens for culinary and medicinal use, and long before synthetic fragrances were first manufactured in the 18th century, perfumes and aromatic cosmetics were made from natural plant material.

Murals and mosaics in Roman villas dating from the 1st century depict scenes of trained vines and gardens full of flowers in bloom, and it is the Romans who spread fragrant herbs like fennel, rosemary and thyme far and wide.

In the Middle Ages, many fragrant plants were grown for nosegays – small bunches of scented flowers and herbs worn on the clothes, or carried to hold under the nose to help mask the everyday odours that were commonplace as a result of poor sanitation and open sewers. It was even thought that bad smells could lead to disease.

Many of the early gardening books celebrated the scent of flowers, foliage and herbs. John Gerard in his *Herball*, published in 1597, described the 'virtues' and folklore surrounding many fragrant herbs used in herbal remedies and recipes.

Field of commercially grown lavender

William Shakespeare often romanticised scented plants in his plays, particularly roses. The Elizabethan gardens familiar to Shakespeare would have been full of sweet-smelling flowers and herbs.

In *A Midsummer Night's Dream*, Oberon says:

'I know a bank where the wild thyme blows,
Where oxlips and the nodding violet grows,
Quite over-canopied with luscious woodbine,
With sweet musk-roses and with eglantine:
There sleeps Titania sometime of the night,
Lulled in these flowers with dances and delight.'

Many modern gardens, although full of colour and with a wide variety of plants, are made up of cultivars and hybrids bred for their hardiness and vigour, often at the expense of the beautiful fragrances, scents and aromas that would have been much more valued in the past.

Annuals, perennials, shrubs and trees can all also add scent to a garden, both through their flowers and their foliage. When I first started working at Kew more than two decades ago, every day I would cycle the same route through the gardens to the area in which I worked, and every time I reached a particular spot I would be stopped by a fragrance in the air that was richly spicey, and would linger to discover where the scent was coming from, but could see nothing flowering close by that might have been the source.

It took me quite a while to realise that the strong aroma was coming not from a flower, but from the foliage of an evergreen shrub called *Escallonia illinita*, specifically from the fallen leaves that surrounded the plant.

It should be noted that scents can be very different to different people, and some of us have trained noses, like those working in perfumery or the production of wines and spirits.

INTRODUCTION

The sense of smell is subjective, so what may be a strong fragrance for some may be only just detected, or not detected at all, by others. I remember an occasion when a friend, Mark Flanagan, who was Keeper of The Gardens at Windsor Great Park, visited me for a walk around Kew's Arboretum. In one particular area we walked past a group of Katsura trees, *Cercidiphyllum japonicum*, where the air was filled with the almost overpowering scent of toffee apples and candyfloss, but surprisingly this could only be picked up by me, even though Mark generally had a good sense of smell for all other plants.

So what exactly is scent? This descriptive word is used here to cover a variety of similar words, such as aroma, fragrance, perfume, smell and odour. While it often describes a pleasant smell, scent can also cover smells that are unpleasant to humans but which are particularly attractive to some insects. Flies, for example, are attracted to the smell of decay, a scent produced by some plants to attract flies and other small creatures, drawing them in for the purposes of pollination.

Scent can be part of a garden's virtues throughout the year, where every month you can have some plants with fragrant flowers, foliage or bark, and in some cases all three.

When thinking of scented plants, we tend to concentrate on flowers and foliage, but other parts of many plants are also scented, for example their fruits. Resins can also add fragrance, like those produced in the leaves of Mediterranean plants like cistus, lavender and rosemary, particularly on warm summer days. Roots and rhizomes can also be aromatic, like those in the ginger family.

I have tried to 'sniff test' every plant mentioned in this book, but some I know from experience, and for those few that I have been unable to personally check, I have relied on other reliable sources, mainly horticultural literature and experienced colleagues.

LEFT
Viburnum x *bodnantense* 'Dawn'

RIGHT
Chimonanthus praecox

Scent

The *Oxford English Dictionary* defines 'scent' as a distinctive smell, especially one that is pleasant. Other words used to describe it include fragrance, perfume and aroma. Odour is another word associated with scent, but it is more usually a scent that is unpleasant.

Often scents can be described differently by different people. For instance, I find the scent of the paper-white daffodil, *Narcissus papyraceus*, very pleasant, and it is often used as a cut flower in southern Spain, but some find its scent unpleasant. I get a chocolatey smell from *Azara microphylla*, but others describe it as being vanilla-scented.

Some scents can be very strong and easily picked up by most people, and often fill the air around the plant, while others are very delicate. In the case of scented foliage, it may need to be rubbed or crushed for the scent to be released.

It is amazing to think that the scent given off from a rose is made up of more than 400 different chemicals, and the flower's association with scent has long been admired.

Anosmia is the inability to smell some things, and this can include detecting smells and odours that are very strong to others. The scent ratings in this book are light, medium and strong, but they are my own labels from what I can detect. This will obviously differ somewhat from other readers' perceptions, and they are only given as a comparison guide between plants.

LEFT
Evening scented
Lonicera periclymenum

RIGHT
English climbing rose
'The Generous Gardener'

Herbs

Herbs are aromatic plants. They may be annuals, biennials, perennials, shrubs, sub-shrubs or trees, and are generally grown in the garden for their culinary or medicinal uses. Although their scents are mainly held within their leaves, when released they are some of the strongest.

Many common herbs store their fragrances as an essential oil within the leaf that they can secrete through glandular hairs on the leaf surface. The pleasant, often soothing aroma is released when the leaf is rubbed, crushed, or brushed against. So herbs are a must in a sensory garden, often stimulating the taste buds too. Many of the Mediterranean herbs have soft, hairy leaves that are an adaptation for drought tolerance, their leaf surface appearing grey or silver with a covering of tiny, fine hairs which both trap moisture and help reflect some of the high levels of heat away from the leaves.

Herbs are also great plants to grow in mixed borders. Many have been grown as cottage garden plants for centuries, and they are great plants for attracting

OPPOSITE LEFT
White-flowered borage
OPPOSITE RIGHT
Delicate small flowers of dill

RIGHT
Flowering spikes of lemon thyme

pollinating insects, such as bees and butterflies. As with most scented plants, the perfume is produced either to attract insects that pollinate their flowers – in order to produce seed for future generations – or to deter insects or animals from eating them.

They are obvious plants for growing together in a herb garden for their medicinal or culinary uses in dishes and herbal teas, close at hand to a kitchen, where they will grow just as well in pots as in the ground, provided they are well watered and cared for.

Herbs have had much folklore attached to them. The ancient Greeks wouldn't eat parsley because they believed that it grew from the blood of Archemorus, a young child who – according to Greek mythology – was killed by a serpent. Instead, they used it to make wreaths for the dead. However, the Romans believed that wearing a garland of parsley during feasting would stop them getting drunk!

Herbs were the household air freshener of the Elizabethan age and were grown in the garden for that purpose. Known as 'strewing herbs', they were strewn on the floors of rooms where they would be crushed when walked upon, releasing their scents and masking disagreeable odours. Some of the best herbs for strewing were described in a 16th-century book by Thomas Tusser titled *Five Hundred Points of Good Husbandry*, including camomile, cowslips, hyssop, lavender, lemon balm, marjoram, mints, tansy and violets, to name just a few.

Although herbs have been popular for their varied uses over many centuries, the availability of modern hybrids and cultivars mean they are as popular as ever today.

Scent and wildlife

As much as we admire the aromas of many of our flowering plants, the main reason that flowers produce scent is to attract pollinating insects. Worldwide, around 75% of all the food we eat is reliant on pollination by animals, including bees and other insects, so scent as one of the attractors is vitally important.

But the scent that plants produce can also work as a repellent to deter herbivores from eating them. This is most usually through scent molecules stored in their leaves and stems, released when these are crushed, which is what happens when animals attempt to eat them.

Flowering plants and their pollinators have co-evolved and are almost totally dependent on each other. By contrast, wind-pollinated plants – such as willows and alders which produce pollen in long catkins – have fine, dust-like pollen that is easily transferred from one plant to another as they sway to and fro, releasing their pollen on the slightest of breezes. Pollen spread by insects, however, ensures cross-pollination to maximise the amount of genetic variation in seeds, which in turn gives plants more resistance to diseases.

The flower scents that attract pollinators are mostly produced from glands on the petal surfaces. These scents, along with colour patterns, advertise a reward of nectar and pollen. When pollinators visit flowers, pollen produced by the anthers – which are the tips of the male stamens – is transferred to the female stigma of another flower. This is an essential process for the plant to produce viable seeds for future generations. The rewards for the pollinators are the proteins, fats and sugars in the pollen, which for bees are food for their developing larvae.

As a beekeeper I have always been fascinated by the variety of different colours of pollen collected by bees, not just from scented plants but from all plants. Pollen grains range from almost black in the oriental poppy, through lots of different shades of red in plants such as gorse, snowdrops and cherries. There is also the green pollen of meadowsweet, the brown pollen of marjoram and a range of yellows, including bluebell and evening primrose pollen.

ABOVE
Bumblebee enjoying some nectar

RIGHT
Red admiral butterfly feeding on the aptly named butterfly bush

It has been estimated that a honeybee colony may collect anything from 15 to 55 kg of pollen per year, which is a staggering amount when you see how little each bee can carry at any one time!

Nectar is also sought by pollinators and is usually produced from the nectaries inside the flower's base, but can also be produced from 'extrafloral nectaries' that occur outside of the flowers, often at the base of leaf stalks. Nectar provides carbohydrates and is the energy food for many insects, including butterflies and all types of bees. But it is only honeybees that convert nectar into honey by adding enzymes to alter its composition and reduce the moisture content. This is their colony's food source throughout the winter months.

Many of today's ornamental flower varieties favour double flowers, having many more petals than the single-flowered forms, which tend to have between four and eight. Some doubles have dozens of petals. One of the issues in producing more petals through breeding is that the flowers' reproductive organs are converted to petals, which makes the plants sterile.

The doubles are often showier and can still be very fragrant, particularly some of the new English rose cultivars, but what they add visually is almost always to the detriment of pollinating insects, especially bees and butterflies, as it can be very difficult for them to access the nectaries, which are reduced by the mutation of all of the extra petals. So single flowers win hands down when it comes to supplying both nectar and pollen. From a gardener's point of view, though, flowers that are sterile and therefore cannot be pollinated last longer in flower, so a mix in a border of both fertile and infertile flowers will keep both the gardeners and the pollinators happy.

Evening-scented flowers like honeysuckles, evening-scented primrose and others have evolved to attract pollinating insects that are active around and after dusk by producing their strong fragrances during this time. Night-flying moths are particularly attracted to many of these flowers along with many other insects, and these in turn are a food source for foraging bats.

Growing a range of different types of scented flowering plants will attract a larger diversity of insects. Flowers with petals that produce long tubes, such as the tobacco plant, will provide nectar for insects with long tongues, including butterflies and moths. Those with more open flowers like heliotropes, *Heliotropium arborescens*, will attract smaller insects.

So as well as adding the sensory interest of scent for yourself in the garden, you will also be benefitting wildlife.

ABOVE
The painted lady butterfly, a summer visitor to the UK

RIGHT
The highly scented *Osmanthus delavayi* attracts a host of different pollinators

Annuals and biennials

Annuals and biennials

There is often debate as to what is a biennial as opposed to a short-lived perennial. To my mind, a plant that is grown from seed, producing its flowers in the second season before dying, is a biennial, whereas a plant that continues to grow for more than the second season is either a short-lived perennial, or simply a perennial if it continues to grow for many seasons.

COTA AUSTRIACA
Corn camomile
ASTERACEAE

Most of the plants in this book have fragrant flowers, but some have aromatic foliage, which is the case with corn camomile, though the foliage has to be bruised to release its aroma.

This plant has had a recent name change from *Anthemis austriaca*.

The flowers of this pretty annual plant are small and daisy-like, borne on branched flowering stalks. As its name suggests, corn camomile was once common in corn fields – along with other wildflowers like corncockle, corn marigolds and poppies – where they were classed as arable weeds.

It is now mainly found as part of wildflower seed mixes and is a good pollen producer, making it an ideal plant for attracting hoverflies and solitary bees.
ASPECT: Full sun or partial shade.
FLOWERING: May–August.
SCENTED FOLIAGE: Medium.
HARDINESS: -10 to -15 °C (14 to 5 °F).

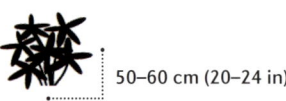 50–60 cm (20–24 in)

30–50 cm (12–20 in)

DIANTHUS BARBATUS
Garden pinks
CARYOPHYLLACEAE

Also known as sweet William, this wonderfully scented plant is technically a short-lived perennial, but is usually treated as a biennial. It produces flowers in a range of colours from white, to red, to purple, some with mixed colours around their border, or a central blotch, usually white, adding to their attraction.

Sweet William was a favourite plant of the old cottage gardens, where it would be part of a mixed planting that would give colour and scent all summer long, often lasting right up until the first frosts.

The flowers can be single or double and are produced on tall, stiff stems, in many-flowered, terminal clusters. The plant is ideal for cutting, bringing scent into the house, as well as in beds, borders and containers.

Deadheading faded flowers regularly will extend the flowering period.
ASPECT: Full sun.
FLOWERING: July–September.
SCENT: Strong.
HARDINESS: -10 to -15 °C (14 to 5 °F).

 25–50 cm (10–20 in)

10–30 cm (4–12 in)

ERYSIMUM CHEIRI
Wallflower
BRASSICACEAE

Wallflowers are another example of a short-lived perennial that is best treated as a biennial, because they become leggy and untidy in their second flowering season. They are also more susceptible to clubroot (a disease of many plants in this family) if grown continually in the same spot.

Cota austriaca

Erysimum 'Rysi Copper'

20 GARDENING WITH SCENTED PLANTS

Wallflowers smell sweetly of cloves and are attractive to bees for both their pollen and their nectar. Their single, four-petalled flowers are produced in small clusters in a variety of colours from yellow to the deepest purples.

My father-in-law was a keen gardener and a market porter in the old Covent Garden flower market, and I can remember each autumn he would bring home bare-rooted wallflowers in bundles of ten wrapped in damp newspaper. These would be planted out in his beds among the roses. Bought and planted this way they will flower a little earlier in the season than smaller, younger plants bought in pots.

Often used in spring bedding, they make a good combination planted with tulips and the blue, low-flowering forget-me-nots.

ASPECT: Full sun.
FLOWERING: April–June.
SCENT: Strong.
HARDINESS: -10 to -15 °C (14 to 5 °F).

 25–50 cm (10–20 in)
10–30 cm (4–12 in)

HELIOTROPIUM ARBORESCENS
Heliotrope

BORAGINACEAE

Grown as a half-hardy annual, heliotrope is a small sub-shrub that is native to South America so not fully hardy in the UK. But it is a plant well worth growing as part of a scented garden as it does well either in containers on a patio or as a plant for the front of an ornamental border.

Grown in a container in a sheltered patio, or in a conservatory, it will live for several seasons.

Small, blue-purple, trumpet-shaped, sweetly scented flowers are produced in dome-shaped branched inflorescences. They are said to smell of cherries and vanilla, hence heliotrope is also known as the cherry pie plant.

Deadheading regularly will encourage repeat flowering over an extended period.
ASPECT: Full sun to partial shade.
FLOWERING: June–October.
SCENT: Medium.
HARDINESS: 1 to -5 °C (34 to 23 °F).

 30–40 cm (12–16 in)
20–30 cm (8–12 in)

IPOMOEA ALBA
Moonflower

CONVOLVULACEAE

The common name for this climbing vine, moonflower, is very apt as it produces large (up to 15 cm or 6 in across), pure white, fragrant flowers that open around dusk and unfurl into flat, round flowers with a pale green star in their throat. They release their fragrance to the night air, before closing as the dawn light begins a new day. New flowers are produced each evening throughout the summer months.

Moonflower grows rapidly from seed and will need a structure or support for its long twining stems to attach themselves to. The stems are clothed in large, heart-shaped leaves. The vine needs a sunny, sheltered spot, greenhouse or conservatory. If it is grown in a large container, a sheltered patio will provide an ideal place to sit and enjoy its evening fragrance.

The more commonly known *Ipomoea purpurea*, morning glory, has purple flowers that open in the morning, as its name suggests, and is not fragrant.

ASPECT: Full sun.
FLOWERING: June–September.
SCENT: Medium.
HARDINESS: 10 to 15 °C (50 to 59 °F).

 2–3 m (6–10 ft)
1–31.5 m (3–5 ft)

Ipomoea alba

ANNUALS AND BIENNIALS 21

LATHYRUS ODORATUS
Sweet pea
FABACEAE

The fragrance of sweet peas is one of the many joys of summer and they are surely the perfect scented climbing annual.

There is a large range of modern cultivars in many colours, mostly pastel shades. Many are bi-coloured, combining two colours within the same flower. Unlike many modern cultivars of other plants, most sweet peas have been bred to retain their fragrance – some more than others, but all are scented.

Their flowers are made up of three main parts, usually all just referred to as petals. The uppermost and largest petal is known as the banner or standard, with the lower petals divided into two parts: the wings, which form a kind of hood, and the keel below the wings. In most bi-coloured flowers it is the banner that differs in colour from the wings and keel.

Examples of popular varieties in particular colours include:

Pure white – *Lathyrus odoratus* 'Valentine', which produces clusters of strongly scented flowers.

Yellow – 'Primrose' is the closest to a yellow, a colour that has been difficult to breed. Its lime green buds open cream and become yellower as the flowers mature.

Lilac – 'Chrissie', which has a good scent, has petals with a marbled colouration but its overall colour is lilac, darkening to a deep lavender as it matures.

Red – 'King Edward VII' – a sweet pea that has been a popular garden plant for more than a century – has a rich red colour with a good strong scent.

Purple – 'Almost black' has a rich scent and the deepest maroon flowers that are, literally, almost black! It is also one of the taller cultivars, reaching around 2.5 m (8 ft).

Bi-coloured – 'Little Red Riding Hood', as its name might suggest, has a red banner above white wings and keel. Its flowers are very strongly scented. 'Cedric Morris' has a very distinct look with a maroon banner and bluish-mauve wings and keel.

Removing the tendrils on most sweet peas will provide more energy for the flowers, producing bigger flowers on longer stalks. However, they will need regular tying into their support, whether that is a trellis, canes, or a pergola.

Picking and cutting the flowers for indoor use, and regular deadheading, will stop them setting seed and greatly extend their flowering. Even a small bunch will fill a room with their wonderful scent.

Sweet peas are prone to mildew so need to be grown in free-draining, moisture-retentive soils that do not dry out. Equally, they will not do well in heavy, wet soils.

Sow seeds in autumn to get earlier flowering.

ASPECT: Full sun.
FLOWERING: June–September.
SCENT: Strong.
HARDINESS: 1 to -5 °C (34 to 23 °F).

 2–5 m (6–8 ft)
20–30 cm (8–12 in)

> Wonderful summer climbing annual, delivering sweet fragrance both in the garden and indoors as cut flowers

Lathyrus 'Primrose'

Lathyrus 'Chrissie'

Lathyrus 'Little Red Riding Hood'

Lathyrus 'Almost Black'

Lobularia maritima

LOBULARIA MARITIMA
Sweet alyssum
BRASSICACEAE

Often also referred to as sweet Alison, this Mediterranean native is also drought-tolerant once established, producing a low-growing carpet of tiny, brilliant white fragrant flowers.

Its low-growing habit makes it an ideal summer bedding plant for the edges of a bed or border. It is also perfect for growing in mixed containers with other taller plants. 'Snowdrift' is a popular cultivar with brilliant white flowers and a good scent.

ASPECT: Full sun to partial shade.
FLOWERING: June–September.
SCENT: Medium.
HARDINESS: 1 to -5 °C (34 to 23 °F).

 10–15 cm (4–6 in)

10–15 cm (4–6 in)

MATTHIOLA LONGIPETALA
Night-scented stock
BRASSICACEAE

This is a perfect plant for a sunny border, preferably one that is close to a seating area where the strong fragrance can be appreciated. Night-scented stocks are best grown as a large group, with the seed sown direct in patches throughout a bed between other plants, as individually they can become leggy and a bit straggly. As a group they will hold each other up and produce more scent.

The dainty, four-petalled flowers are generally lilac-coloured, but can also be pink or white, contrasting well with the glaucous green foliage. They are not the showiest of flowers, but you will be rewarded with their delicious summer fragrance.

Removing the spent flowers ensures that more new flowers will be continuously produced.

ASPECT: Full sun.
FLOWERING: April–July.
SCENT: Medium.
HARDINESS: 1 to -5 °C (34 to 23 °F).

 20–30 cm (8–12 in)

20–30 cm (8–12 in)

MIRABILIS JALAPA
Four o'clock flower
NYCTAGINACEAE

Also known as the marvel of Peru, *Mirabilis jalapa* was once a lot more commonly grown and was a favourite of the Victorians.

Cultivated as a half-hardy annual, often in summer bedding schemes, it has succulent-looking stems and dark green leaves that produce a bushy plant, with trumpet-shaped, fragrant flowers that are a mix of colours in shades of red, crimson, orange and white. Some of the flowers are also bicoloured.

The flowers open each afternoon (at around 4pm as their common name suggests) and flower right through the night, continuing to produce their heady scent.

If grown in a pot, *Mirabilis jalapa* can be treated as a tender perennial and will produce a small tuber. Kept frost-free over winter in a greenhouse or conservatory, its tuber will get bigger each year, producing an earlier flowering plant in the late spring.

ASPECT: Full sun.
FLOWERING: June–August.
SCENT: Strong.
HARDINESS: 1 to -5 °C (34 to 23 °F).

 50–70 cm (20–28 in)

40–60 cm (16–24 in)

Mirabilis jalapa

NICOTIANA ALATA
Jasmine tobacco
SOLANACEAE

Nicotiana is a genus of around 50 different species, only one of which is commonly used to produce tobacco. Though most are scented, *Nicotiana alata* is by far the most fragrant.

Producing masses of flowers in a variety of colours, including white, pink and red, it can also be green, which is my personal favourite. Apart from the colour, they all have very similar, five-petalled, star-shaped, long, trumpet-like flowers, produced on a tall flowering spike above a basal rosette of leaves.

They look really good when planted as mixed colours in a cottage garden or as a group in a herbaceous border. They also make good container plants.

Only mildly scented through the day, their scent increases into the evening and night.

Like most annuals, deadheading spent flowers will increase their flowering period.

ASPECT: Full sun to partial shade.
FLOWERING: May–October.
SCENT: Strong.
HARDINESS: 1 to -5 °C (34 to 23 °F).

1–1.5 m (3–5 ft)

30–50 cm (12–20 in)

Nicotiana alata

OENOTHERA BIENNIS
Evening primrose
ONAGRACEAE

Evening primrose is a biennial, so its pretty, pale-yellow flowers are produced in the second year when they give off their delicate fragrance around dusk. The large flowers are borne on tall, hairy stems (that are often purple-tinged) throughout the summer months.

New flowers open each evening, and remain open until the following morning, making evening primrose an ideal flowering plant that provides a good source of nectar for bees and butterflies during daylight and moths after dark, so a great addition to a wildlife garden.

The behaviour of plants like the evening primrose whose flowers open at night is known as nyctinasty.

Commercially, evening primrose oil from the mature seeds is processed into cosmetics and skincare products.

ASPECT: Full sun to partial shade.
FLOWERING: June–September.
SCENT: Medium.
HARDINESS: -10 to -15 °C (14 to 5 °F).

0.5–1 m (20–40 in)

10–50 cm (4–20 in)

Oenothera biennis

Reseda odorata

RESEDA ODORATA
Mignonette
RESEDACEAE

This plant's common name, mignonette, is French for 'little darling', presumably because of its sweet fragrance.

Once commonly grown as a cottage garden plant, mignonette grows a tall, erect, branching stem, with unusual-looking flowers that have tiny white or yellowish petals and numerous showy orange anthers. It is a great bee plant.

Mignonette has had many uses over the centuries. The Romans used it as a treatment for bruises, for example. It can be turned into a yellow dye and has also been cultivated commercially for its essential oils, which are used in perfumery. Cut and dried, the fragrance of mignonette will keep for months and so it is often used in pot pourri.

ASPECT: Full sun or partial shade.
FLOWERING: June–October.
SCENT: Medium.
HARDINESS: -10 to -15 °C (14 to 5 °F).

30–50 cm (12–20 in)

30–50 cm (12–20 in)

ANNUALS AND BIENNIALS 25

Bulbs

Bulbs

This section covers bulbs, corms, rhizomes and tubers. Each plant profile will state which type applies.

ALLIUM URSINUM
Wild garlic
AMARYLLIDACEAE

I remember the first time I came across wild garlic growing in a woodland in South Wales, I smelt the plants long before I saw them, a carpet of white. Wild garlic, also known as ransoms, covered much of the woodland floor and obviously some had been trodden on, releasing their pungent scent.

The fresh green leaves emerge just before a single flower spike is produced, topped by a rounded cluster of around 25 small, white, star-shaped flowers.

In addition to its scent, this plant has the bonus that all of its parts are edible.

Wild garlic is such a pretty plant, especially when grown in a shady spot, but it should be grown with caution as it can be quick to spread, via both seeds and bulbils.

ASPECT: Partial shade to full sun.
FLOWERING: March–May.
SCENT: Strong.
HARDINESS: -10 to -15 °C (14 to 5 °F).

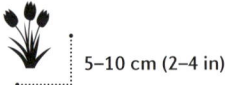
5–10 cm (2–4 in)

10 cm (4 in)

Allium ursinum

CARDIOCRINUM GIGANTEUM
Giant Himalayan lily
LILIACEAE

As its name suggests, this is a plant that can grow to giant proportions, in some cases up to 4 m (13 ft) tall, but more commonly around half that. The giant Himalayan lily is 'monocarpic' (it flowers and sets seed only once), so the original bulb will die after the plant has flowered, but it will have produced offsets that will in time also flower, as well as seed spread from the attractive, elongated seed heads.

The tall flower spike emerges from the centre of a rosette of large, dark green, glossy leaves, and produces around 20 or more large, trumpet-like, downward-facing, cream-coloured and fragrant flowers that have maroon markings in their throat.

After the original bulb has died, the plants take 5–7 years to flower from its offsets and seed, but over time they should build up a colony with some flowering spikes each year.

ASPECT: Partial shade.
FLOWERING: June–July.
SCENT: Medium.
HARDINESS: -5 to -10 °C (23 to 14 °F).

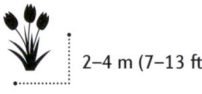
2–4 m (7–13 ft)

30 cm (12 in)

Cardiocrinum giganteum

CHLIDANTHUS FRAGRANS
Perfumed fairy lily
AMARYLLIDACEAE

This is a rare and unusual, fragrant summer-flowering bulb. As it is half hardy and might not survive in the ground over a cold wet winter, it is best grown in a conservatory or a container that can be placed on a patio near a seating area where the fragrance of its sweetly scented flowers can be enjoyed.

The vibrant, golden-yellow, trumpet-shaped flowers are borne in small clusters on upright stems in early to mid-summer.

ASPECT: Full sun to partial shade.
FLOWERING: June–July.
SCENT: Medium.
HARDINESS: 5 to 10 °C (41 to 50 °F).

20–30 cm (8–12 in)

5–10 cm (2–4 in)

CONVALLARIA MAJALIS
Lily of the valley
ASPARAGACEAE

Found growing naturally in ancient woodland, this pretty little plant, also known as May bells, is native to much of Europe including Great Britain. It produces a flowering spike between a pair of large, oval leaves. Its sweetly fragrant flowers are white, bell-shaped, with petals that turn up at the opening. Up to 15 individual flowers are produced and are followed by small, orange-red berries.

Lily of the valley doesn't make a bulb, but grows from spreading underground rhizomes, and is ideal for growing in a damp, shady border where it will spread and make an attractive, scented groundcover. It also makes an excellent cut flower, often used in bouquets.

There is also a much less common pink variety, *Convallaria majalis* var. *rosea*, which is equally fragrant.

ASPECT: Partial–full shade.
FLOWERING: April–May.
SCENT: Medium.
HARDINESS: -10 to -15 °C (14 to 5° F).

15–25 cm (6–10 in)

30 cm (12 in)

FREESIA REFRACTA
Freesia
IRIDACEAE

This is a wonderfully fragrant plant produced from a corm. Its flowering stem bears around 5 to 10 creamy-white or pale-yellow, funnel-shaped flowers that are tinged with purple and are produced loosely along a one-sided flowering spike.

Chlidanthus fragrans

Convallaria majalis

BULBS 29

I first came across this plant growing as an escapee in Gibraltar where it was flourishing among limestone rocks, its scent absolutely filling the surrounding air.

I have seen it growing in gardens in Britain, but it is not fully hardy, so should only be tried outside in a sheltered, sunny site with very free-draining soil. An ideal site would probably be in a rockery. Grown in containers in a conservatory or frost-free greenhouse, you will be rewarded by its heady fragrance. It also makes a very good cut flower.

You can buy corms that have been heat-treated, which mimics their native South African summer, but they generally have a short life, maybe flowering only once.

ASPECT: Full sun.
FLOWERING: April–May.
SCENT: Strong.
HARDINESS: 1 to 5 °C (14 to 5 °F).

25–30 cm (10–12 in)
10 cm (4 in)

Galanthus elwesii 'S. Arnott'

FRITILLARIA IMPERIALIS
Crown imperial
LILIACEAE

Crown imperials are truly impressive, even more so if they are grown as a group, when their tall flowering stems make a bold statement, some growing to over a metre in height.

Each large, fist-sized bulb produces a single stem, topped with a terminal cluster of big, bell-shaped orange or yellow flowers, with exposed stigmas and anthers beneath a head of green, leaf-like bracts.

There is one drawback with this striking plant and that is its unusual fragrance, which can be best described as musk-like and slightly unpleasant. So it is probably not one to plant too close to a seating area!

There are many cultivars available with colours ranging from cream through to deep reds.

ASPECT: Full sun to partial shade.
FLOWERING: April–May.
SCENT: Strong.
HARDINESS: -10 to -15 °C (14 to 5 °F).

60 cm–1 m (2–3 ft)
20–30 cm (8–12 in)

GALANTHUS ELWESII 'S. ARNOTT'
Snowdrop
AMARYLLIDACEAE

One of the floral pleasures as winter turns to spring is the nodding, flowering heads of snowdrops. They bring such joy at a time of year when there is little else flowering – a sign of things to come that is soon followed by a flush of other colour and scent.

Galanthus elwesii 'S. Arnott' has fragrant, honey-scented white flowers, each with a thin V-shaped mark on the tips of the inner segment and pure white outer petals. Grown as a large group, its scent can be enjoyed on the warmer days of winter.

This cultivar has been around a long time. It was introduced in the 19th century after being found by a keen gardener, Samuel Arnott, growing in his garden.

It will spread vegetatively so is a good choice for naturalising and planting or dividing clumps, which is always best done when 'in the green'.

ASPECT: Partial shade to full sun.
FLOWERING: February–March.
SCENT: Medium.
HARDINESS: -10 to -15 °C (14 to 5 °F).

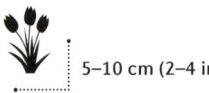
5–10 cm (2–4 in)
10 cm (4 in)

OPPOSITE
Fritillaria imperialis

GLADIOLUS MURIELAE
Abyssinian gladiolus
IRIDACEAE

Produced from a corm, this elegant plant is best grown in a group or drifts in a sunny border where its late-summer flowers will help hold each other up as they move around in the breeze.

The white, star-shaped flowers are marked with a maroon blotch at the base of each petal and are borne on spikes above their tall, strap-like leaves, where each flower nods gracefully.

The beautifully fragrant flowers grow well in containers as well as in the ground and make a good cut flower, producing a long-lasting bloom with a wonderful vanilla scent.

ASPECT: Full sun.
FLOWERING: August–October.
SCENT: Medium.
HARDINESS: -1 to -5 °C (30 to 23 °F).

0.5–1 m (1.5–3 ft)
10 cm (4 in)

HEMEROCALLIS LILIOASPHODELUS
Yellow daylily
ASPHODELACEAE

Spreading via its rhizomes, the yellow daylily will increase happily, eventually growing into large clumps and producing masses of bright, lemon-yellow, trumpet-shaped flowers. These are sweetly fragrant and held above the plant's narrow, strap-like leaves, which are semi-evergreen, staying green in mild winters.

The main flush of flowers open after midday and each flower only lasts one day (sometimes two), as its common and Latin names suggest (*Hemerocallis* means beautiful for a day). But new flowers are continually produced in early summer and regular deadheading will prolong flowering.

Once it has finished, cut back the old flowering stems and remove dead foliage in late autumn if needed. Dividing clumps every 3 or 4 years will keep them growing vigorously.

ASPECT: Full sun.
FLOWERING: May–June.
SCENT: Medium.
HARDINESS: -10 to -15 °C (14 to 5 °F).

50–75 cm (1.5–2.5 ft)
75 cm (2–5 ft)

Gladiolus murielae

Hemerocallis lilioasphodelus

32   GARDENING WITH SCENTED PLANTS

Hyacinthoides non-scripta

HYACINTHOIDES NON-SCRIPTA
Common bluebell
ASPARAGACEAE

The common bluebell brings a woodland to life, creating a wildflower spectacle in spring before the trees come into leaf and cast their shade across the plants below.

It is a plant that is surrounded by folklore and has many common names, such as fairy flower, lady's nightcap and witches' thimbles. Entering a woodland carpeted with the flowers' blue haze is certainly enchanting. Sometimes pink and white flowers will also be seen.

Individually, their sweet scent is quite faint, so to be enjoyed they must be *en masse*. The violet-blue, bell-shaped flowers are produced on a one-sided, drooping stem of around 15 individual flowers. Each has six petals that are turned up at their tips and creamy coloured anthers, which distinguishes them from hybrid and Spanish bluebells, which have an upright stem, bluish anthers and are not fragrant.

These are a great plant for a woodland area of a garden and their early flowering makes them of considerable benefit to wildlife. They will readily – if slowly – spread via their seed and bulbils to form small, dense clumps.

ASPECT: Partial shade to full sun.
FLOWERING: April–May.
SCENT: Light.
HARDINESS: -10 to -15 °C (14 to 5 °F).

 30–40 cm (12–16 in)
15 cm (6 in)

HYACINTHUS ORIENTALIS
Common hyacinth
ASPARAGACEAE

The common hyacinth is most commonly grown for its striking colours and scent as a pot plant or in containers for indoors. But it can also be grown outdoors, either in mixed containers for an early spring display or planted in the ground in autumn for flowering the following spring with other bulbs. It needs to be in a free-draining soil, so that it doesn't sit in cold wet conditions over winter.

Hyacinths come in a range of colours from white, pink and red to various shades of purple and blue. Each bulb produces a dense spike of tubular, waxy, bell-shaped flowers with a rich fragrance. The flower spike sits neatly above the plant's thick, glossy, bright green leaves.

Hyacinths will generally only last 3 or 4 years, but will produce bulblets so should continue producing new flowering plants close to the parent plants.

ASPECT: Full sun–partial shade.
FLOWERING: March–April.
SCENT: Strong.
HARDINESS: -10 to -15 °C (14 to 5 °F).

 25–30 cm (10–12 in)
15 cm (6 in)

LILIUM CANDIDUM
Madonna lily
LILIACEAE

The Madonna lily has been cultivated for millennia, appearing in the famous Minoan fresco 'Prince of the Lilies', which was created around 1,500 BCE. It is still admired by florists for its pure white, scented flowers.

The large, trumpet-shaped flowers have showy bright yellow stamens that stand out well against the white of the flowers and add to their attractiveness. They are borne on tall, stiff stems, producing up to ten individual blooms.

They prefer a spot that doesn't sit in full sun all day, so a sheltered place alongside a pathway where you can enjoy their fragrance would be ideal.

Once flowering is over in autumn, cut the stems down to ground level.

ASPECT: Partial shade to full sun.
FLOWERING: June–August.
SCENT: Strong.
HARDINESS: -10 to -15 °C (14 to 5 °F).

 1–1.5 m (3–5 ft)
30–50 cm (12–20 in)

Hyacinthus orientalis

BULBS 33

LILIUM MARTAGON
Martagon lily
LILIACEAE

As a native of summer meadows in the mountains of Switzerland, the Martagon lily can cope with growing in full sun, though it performs better in a sheltered spot with dappled shade. This makes it ideal for growing in a woodland garden, but it will also grow well in a container and makes an excellent cut flower.

It is also commonly known as the Turk's cap lily due to the shape of its flowers: as they open and mature the petals become totally recurved, resembling a Turkish turban, their showy orange stamens protruding below.

The fragrant flowers usually have purplish-pink petals that are patterned with darker spots, and are borne downward-facing on tall, slender, stiff stems that hang like lanterns.

Once flowering is over in autumn, cut the stems down to ground level.
ASPECT: Full sun to partial shade.
FLOWERING: June–July.
SCENT: Medium.
HARDINESS: -10 to -15 °C (14 to 5 °F).

1–1.2 m (3–4 ft)

30–50 cm (12–20 in)

LILIUM REGALE
Regal lily
LILIACEAE

I can only imagine what it must have been like for the early plant hunters to come across this plant for the first time. They may have picked up its fragrance in the air even before they saw it!

Each huge bulb sends up a flower spike up to 1.5 m (5 ft) tall. Occasionally they can reach 2 m (6 ft 7 in). Each flowering spike produces up to 15 enormous, trumpet-shaped flowers, which are a deep pink when in bud and open white with a yellow throat, retaining their pink bud colour on the backs of the petals.

Regal lilies are best planted in groups in a sunny border, but they will do equally well grown in containers and make an excellent cut flower. A single stem will fill a room with its heady fragrance.

Once flowering has finished in autumn, cut the spent stems back to ground level.
ASPECT: Full sun to partial shade.
FLOWERING: June–July.
SCENT: Strong.
HARDINESS: -10 to -15 °C (14 to 5 °F).

1–1.5 m (3–5 ft)

20–50 cm (8–18 in)

Lilium martagon

Lilium regale

Narcissus

Daffodils are a great choice for not only adding scent, but also early colour to the garden, with a wide range of varieties that flower from early winter, right up until late spring. Their scented blooms have a rich and spicy fragrance or are sweetly perfumed.

Most will do equally well whether planted in containers or in beds and borders, where they mix well between shrubs and with other spring-flowering bulbs like tulips and hyacinths. They are also ideal for indoors, where their fragrance can be enjoyed either as pot plants or cut flowers.

The later-flowering poeticus types are ideal for naturalising and the single-flowered types are a great food source for early pollinating insects, particularly bees.

NARCISSUS JONQUILLA
Scented jonquil
AMARYLLIDACEAE

I have been fortunate enough to see this wonderful little daffodil growing wild *en masse* along the edges of roadsides and fields in southern Spain. Each of the golden-yellow flowers has six petals surrounding a small, central, shallowly lobed cup. The flowers are heavily scented and each is held on a long, slightly upturned tube, making them stand out from the main stem, which usually bears up to five flowers but often more.

They are also known as the rush daffodil due to the shape of their rounded leaves.

Like many bulbs, they will grow in the ground or in containers. They multiply well, so overcrowded clumps should be divided in autumn.

Narcissus jonquilla

Do not cut back foliage until it has become withered and yellow. This allows the leaves to continue to feed the bulb for the following year's flowering.
ASPECT: Full sun to partial shade.
FLOWERING: March–April.
SCENT: Medium.
HARDINESS: -10 to -15 °C (14 to 5 °F).

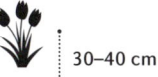

30–40 cm (12–16 in)
10 cm (4 in)

NARCISSUS PAPYRACEUS
Paper-white narcissus
AMARYLLIDACEAE

This daffodil has a lot going for it. Although native to the Mediterranean, I have found it to be extremely hardy. It is often listed as not hardy, but for more than ten years I have grown it in my own garden and the Mediterranean Garden at Kew, where it has endured temperatures regularly below freezing and down to as low as -7 °C.

Narcissus papyraceus

Paper-white narcissus produces up to ten small, pure white, fragrant flowers on a stem. Plant them in small groups to create the best display. The groups will slowly increase, and after time can be divided and spread around the garden or planted in pots, where they will do equally well.

They have a really long flowering period and can be in flower from as early as late November right through until the beginning of March. They make excellent cut flowers, filling a room with their strong fragrance.

Do not cut back the foliage until it has become withered and yellow. This allows the leaves to continue to feed the bulb for the following year's flowering.
ASPECT: Full sun to partial shade.
FLOWERING: December–March.
SCENT: Strong.
HARDINESS: -5 to -10 °C (23 to 14 °F).

30–40 cm (12–16 in)
10 cm (4 in)

BULBS 35

NARCISSUS POETICUS
Pheasant's eye daffodil
AMARYLLIDACEAE

This is a small, sweetly scented daffodil – another wonderfully attractive species in the genus narcissus. It does particularly well in pots and containers, as well as in beds, and is very good for naturalising in grass areas, producing drifts that work well following on in areas planted with the wild daffodil, *Narcissus pseudonarcissus*.

It produces solitary flowers with pure white, recurved petals that grow back away from its small, yellow, central cup. This has a distinct, fringed red or orange rim.

Do not cut back foliage until it has become withered and yellow. This allows the leaves to continue to feed the bulb for the following year's flowering.

ASPECT: Full sun to partial shade.
FLOWERING: March–May.
SCENT: Strong.
HARDINESS: -5 to -10 °C (23 to 14 °F).

30–40 cm (12–16 in)
10 cm (4 in)

NARCISSUS TAZETTA
Bunch-flowered narcissus
AMARYLLIDACEAE

Wild forms of this distinctive little daffodil have white petals and an orange or yellowish cup. Heads of up to six or more fragrant flowers are produced on which the petals become reflex as they age.

There are many different cultivars that vary greatly in both size and appearance, but all of are highly fragrant, like 'Martinette' which has clusters of four or five flowers with yellow petals and an orange cup. 'Avalanche' carries more flowers on a taller stem – ten or more on each 40 cm (16 in) stem – that have white petals and a lemon-yellow cup. Then there is 'Minnow', which as its name suggests is a small cultivar around 20 cm (8 in) tall, and has cream-coloured petals with a bright yellow cup.

ASPECT: Full sun to partial shade.
FLOWERING: March–May.
SCENT: Strong.
HARDINESS: -5 to -10 °C (23 to 14 °F).

30–40 cm (12–16 in)
10 cm (4 in)

NARCISSUS 'GRAND SOLEIL D'OR'
AMARYLLIDACEAE

Narcissus 'Grand Soleil d'Or' produces small clusters of scented flowers, 10–20 on each stem. It grows from a bulb that is often used for forcing so that it flowers during the winter as an indoor container plant. But it will also do well growing outdoors if planted in autumn for an early spring flowering.

The flowers have golden-yellow petals, each with a white tip, and bright orange cups. They are produced on tall, slender stems.

Ideally the bulbs should be planted in a free-draining soil so that they don't sit wet during the cold winter months. So a sunny spot in a rock garden or an outdoor container mixed with other spring-flowering plants is a good position. The flowers are also excellent for cutting for a scented indoor display.

Allow the leaves to die back naturally before removing them.

ASPECT: Full sun to partial shade.
FLOWERING: March–April.
SCENT: Medium.
HARDINESS: -5 to -10 °C (23 to 14 °F).

35–45 cm (14–18 in)
10 cm (4 in)

Narcissus poeticus

Narcissus tazetta

ORNITHOGALUM CANDICANS
Summer hyacinth
ASPARAGACEAE

The summer hyacinth originated in South Africa where it was first described as *Hyacinthus candicans* in 1870. It was renamed *Galtonia candicans* but recently changed its name again – to *Ornithogalum candicans* – although it may still be found under other names!

Ornithogalum candicans has flowering spikes that can grow up to 1 m tall, arising from thick, glaucous green, strap-shaped leaves. Up to 30 large, pure white, bell-shaped flowers hang out from the main stem on long, green peduncles. The lower flowers open first, the others gradually following towards the top.

Each bulb produces more than one flowering spike during the summer, giving it a long season of interest. The flowers are only slightly fragrant so it is best to plant the bulbs in groups – they will not only smell more strongly but also look striking among other herbaceous plants in a border. The late summer flowers can also extend your border's season.

Summer hyacinths are fully hardy but need a well-drained soil so the bulbs don't sit wet in winter, as freezing soils will damage them. If this is likely, lift the bulbs in late autumn.

Their leaves can become untidy, though this isn't an issue when they are grown among other plants and they can be left.

ASPECT: Full sun to partial shade.
FLOWERING: July–September.
SCENT: Light.
HARDINESS: -10 to -15 °C (14 to 5 °F).

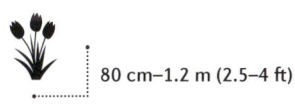

80 cm–1.2 m (2.5–4 ft)
40 cm (16 in)

Ornithogalum candicans

BULBS   37

POLYGONATUM ODORATUM
Scented Solomon's seal
ASPARAGACEAE

Scented Solomon's seal is an ideal plant for growing in a shady area of the garden where its graceful, arching stems look particularly good as ground cover, its creeping rhizomes slowly spreading below small trees and shrubs. The plants do best in heavier, moisture-retentive soils but will tolerate some dryness.

The small, creamy-white, tubular and fragrant flowers are tipped with green and hang in twos and threes on small, drooping stems from each leaf node.

The greyish-white, caterpillar-like larvae of the polygonatum sawfly can be an issue in early summer, feeding on the leaves. In a bad infestation they can defoliate a small group of plants very quickly, though the plants usually recover ready for the following season.

Leave the plant to die down naturally when it has finished flowering.

ASPECT: Partial shade to full sun.
FLOWERING: April–June.
SCENT: Light.
HARDINESS: -10 to -15 °C (14 to 5 °F).

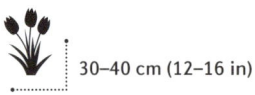

30–40 cm (12–16 in)
30 cm (12 in)

TULBAGHIA VIOLACEA
Society garlic
AMARYLLIDACEAE

This bulbous plant produces large heads of lilac-pink flowers in umbels that sit high above its glaucous green leaves. It flowers for a very long period from early summer until well into the autumn. All parts of the plant are edible and smell and taste mildly of garlic – apparently without leaving you with garlic breath!

It is drought-tolerant, so ideal for growing in a gravel bed with Mediterranean plants that will also enjoy those conditions.

A native of southern Africa, *Tulbaghia* is not fully hardy, although it will take quite a few degrees of frost.

The plants will produce clumps relatively quickly and can be divided if needed in spring.

ASPECT: Full sun.
FLOWERING: March–September.
SCENT: Strong.
HARDINESS: 1 to -5 °C (34 to 23 °F).

30–40 cm (12–16 in)
10 cm (4 in)

Polygonatum odoratum

Tulbaghia violacea

38 GARDENING WITH SCENTED PLANTS

TULIPA SYLVESTRIS
Wild tulip
LILIACEAE

In early spring, the lemon-scented, bright yellow flowers of the wild tulip are a delight in the garden. These cheerful blooms shine on sunny days like oversized, star-shaped buttercups.

Being a species tulip, it tends to be shorter than most of the tall, upright cultivars, but this is its beauty, especially when grown in a rock garden where its lower profile is well suited.

It will naturalise in grass, where it will spread both by seed and underground stolons, and will also happily tolerate some shade.

Leave it to die down naturally when it has finished flowering.

ASPECT: Full sun.
FLOWERING: March–April.
SCENT: Light.
HARDINESS: -10 to -15 °C (14 to 5 °F).

10–20 cm (4–8 in)
20 cm (8 in)

Like yellow shining stars the flowers of this wild tulip are best grown in a container or rock garden for best effect

Tulipa sylvestris

Tulip hybrids

TULIPA HYBRIDS AND CULTIVARS

There are thousands of tulip hybrids and cultivars, but very few that are actually scented. Those listed below are all scented and will do equally well planted in beds or in containers.

'Bellona' – fragrant, cupped yellow blooms – single early.

'Monte Carlo' – bright yellow, honey-scented – double early.

'Princess Irene' – bright orange and burgundy, spicy scent – single early.

'Angélique' – pink and white with a sweet scent – double late.

'Ballerina' – a rich orange lily-flowering tulip with a sweet fragrance.

'Orange Princess' – warm orange with darker makings to the outside petals and a light, honey scent – double late.

'Verona' – creamy-yellow petals and a lemony scent

DARWIN HYBRIDS

The Darwin hybrids are particularly good as they produce large blooms on tall stems that are ideal for cutting. Also known as perennial tulips, they should continue to flower for two or more seasons when planted in free-draining soil in a sunny position.

The following are all sweetly scented:

'Ad Rem' – scarlet red, with golden-yellow edges.

'Apeldoorn' – vibrant scarlet red.

'Golden Apeldoorn' – golden-yellow.

Seedheads on tulips should be removed if possible, as this will allow energy to be used to strengthen the bulbs, but the leaves should be left to die back naturally.

ASPECT: Full sun.
FLOWERING: April–May.
SCENT: Light–medium.
HARDINESS: -10 to -15 °C (14 to 5 °F).

30–50 cm (12–20 in)
10 cm (4 in)

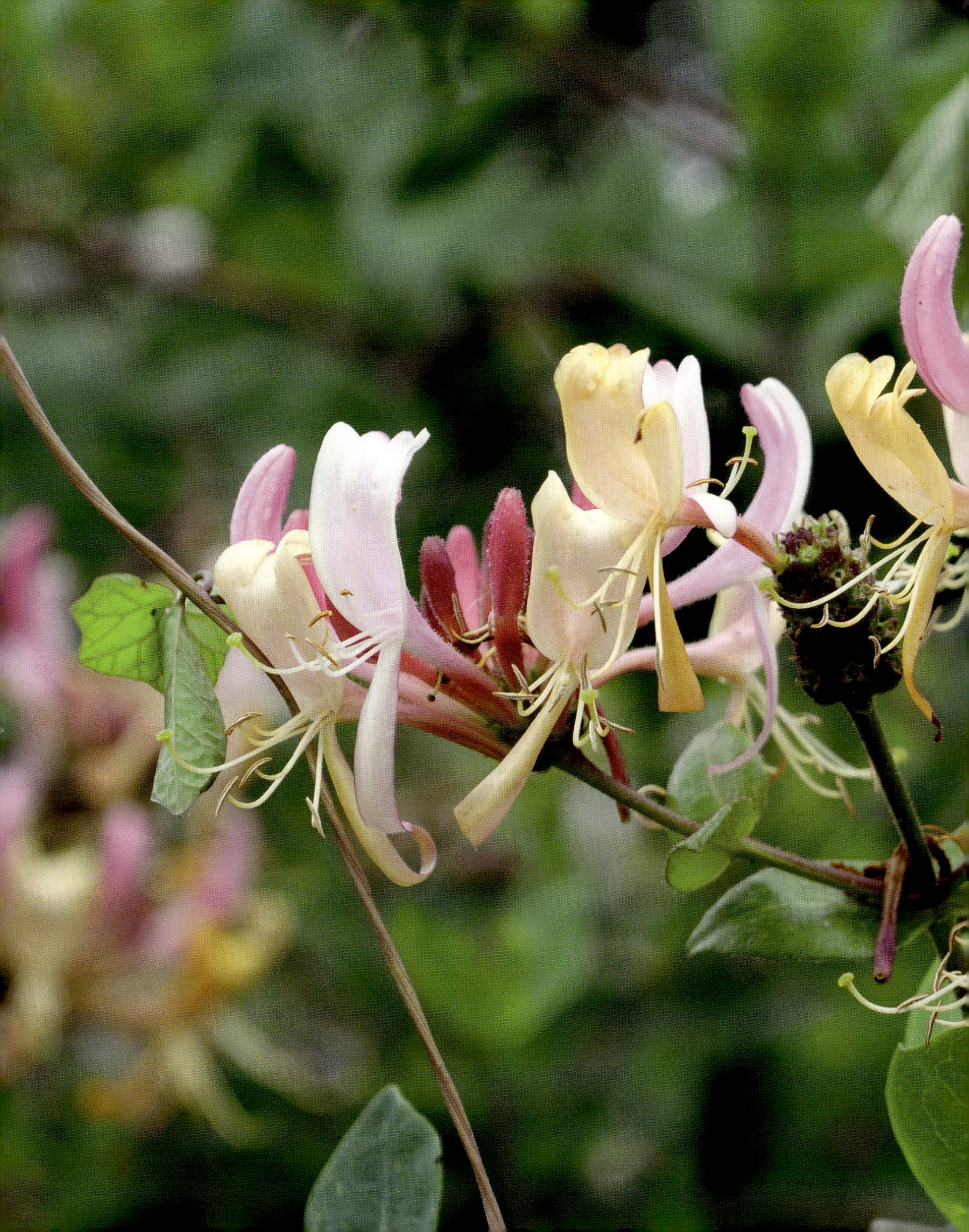

Climbers

AKEBIA QUINATA
Chocolate vine
LARDIZABALACEAE

The chocolate vine is a great semi-evergreen climber for a sheltered, sunny spot. Although the plant itself is quite hardy, the flowers – which are produced early in the year – are prone to being caught by frost. This can also affect the soft growing tips in a severe winter. It is a vigorous climber that will cover an arbour, fence or wall relatively quickly, but will need to be given support to climb on. Its three-lobed leaves are bright green and a good contrast to the dark maroon, vanilla-scented flowers. These look quite unusual, with three bowl-shaped, thick, waxy petals and rounded, protruding stamens in the centre.

There is also a cream-coloured variety.

Chocolate vines can be a little 'shy', often hiding their flowers among the foliage. If there is a second plant for pollination, sausage-like fruits can be produced in hot summers.

Light pruning is all that is needed, cutting out any dead growths, and this should be carried out during the winter.

ASPECT: Full sun to partial shade.
FLOWERING: March–May.
SCENT: Strong.
HARDINESS: -5 to -10 °C (23 to 14 °F).

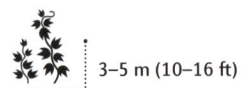

3–5 m (10–16 ft)
3–4 m (10–13 ft)

Akebia quinata

Akebia quinata cream variety

CLEMATIS ARMANDII
Armand clematis
RANUNCULACEAE

A vigorous, evergreen climber with large, glossy, lance-shaped, waxy leaves that are bronze-tinted when young. Clusters of almond-scented, star-like, creamy-white flowers cover the whole of the plant when in full bloom. Armand clematis will be at its best when grown on a sheltered, sunny south- or southwest-

Clematis armandii 'Apple Blossom'

Clematis cirrhosa

CLEMATIS FLAMMULA
Fragrant virgin's bower
RANUNCULACEAE

A large and vigorous, semi-evergreen climber that is deciduous in the coldest winters, producing glossy, dark green, divided leaves followed by masses of pure white, four-petalled, single star-like flowers with an abundance of showy stamens. They have a strong fragrance that is particularly powerful on still summer evenings.

Clematis flammula is ideal for covering walls and fences, but grows equally well through small trees or large shrubs. The flowers are followed by silky seed heads, which extend the season of interest.

This is a late-flowering clematis so should be pruned hard, back to the lowest pair of healthy buds around 15–30 cm (6 in–1 ft) above soil level. This encourages new growth lower down, which will produce flowers. Left unpruned, this clematis will become a tangled mess with most of the flowers high up.

facing wall, with some trellis or wires for its twining stems to attach to. It is a great plant for covering an unsightly wall or fence.

The cultivar **'Apple Blossom'** produces rich, pink buds that are paler pink when they open, eventually becoming white as they mature.

This clematis does not respond well to hard pruning, so it should be pruned annually, thinning out after flowering in mid- to late spring.

ASPECT: Full sun.
FLOWERING: March–April.
SCENT: Strong.
HARDINESS: -5 to -10 °C (23 to 14 °F).

3–5 m (10–16 ft)
2–3 m (7–10 ft)

CLEMATIS CIRRHOSA
Evergreen clematis
RANUNCULACEAE

A favourite of mine as it is one I have seen growing naturally in the wild, where it climbs through the tall shrubs of the garrigue of southern Spain. There it is also known as Spanish traveller's joy, for its pretty flowers and large, showy, fluffy and silky seed heads.

The fragrant flowers are bell-shaped, usually cream-coloured, often with reddish-brown, freckled blotches on the inside of their petals. There are named cultivars like **'Freckles'**, which is particularly well freckled, or **'Jingle Bells'**, which has pure white flowers.

Evergreen clematis is very early flowering, blooming throughout the winter months both sides of Christmas and so is particularly good for any bees, such as bumblebees, that venture out to forage on mild winter days.

Very little pruning is required, apart from tidying any dead or damaged growths and to manage its height or spread. This is best done immediately after flowering.

ASPECT: Full sun to partial shade.
FLOWERING: November–March.
SCENT: Medium.
HARDINESS: -5 to -10 °C (23 to 14 °F).

2–3 m (7–10 ft)
2–3 m (7–10 ft)

Clematis flammula

CLIMBERS

ASPECT: Full sun to partial shade.
FLOWERING: July–September.
SCENT: Strong.
HARDINESS: -5 to -10 °C (23 to 14 °F).

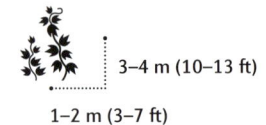

3–4 m (10–13 ft)
1–2 m (3–7 ft)

CLEMATIS MONTANA
Himalayan clematis
RANUNCULACEAE

This is a great clematis for covering up unsightly fences and walls as it is very vigorous, making it an excellent screening plant. Because of its vigour, however, it can become quite dense and heavy, so suitable support is needed.

Depending on the cultivar, the flower colour ranges from pure white, for example **'Grandiflora'**, deep pink, such as **'Warwickshire Rose'**, or the paler pink of **'Pink Perfection'**, which has a delightful fragrance. **'Rubens'**, too, has a pleasing scent.

This is the best clematis for abundance of flowers, with hundreds of flowers covering mature plants. They are four-petalled, with showy central stamens.

There are cultivars and varieties that have been bred to be less rampant, making them more suited to smaller gardens, like *Clematis* **'Freda'**, which has blooms that are mauve pink with darker edges and a light fragrance.

Any pruning that is required – which will mainly be to tidy and reduce its size – should be carried out immediately after flowering has finished.

ASPECT: Full sun to partial shade.
FLOWERING: April–June.
SCENT: Light to medium.
HARDINESS: -5 to -10 °C (23 to 14 °F).

4–8 m (13–26 ft)
2–3 m (7–10 ft)

Clematis montana

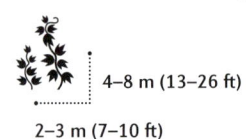

CLEMATIS REHDERIANA
Nodding virgin's bower
RANUNCULACEAE

A deciduous climber that will come into its own late in the season, flowering from mid-summer until early autumn. Like most clematis it will need support to climb and is a good candidate for growing on a north-facing wall or fence.

It is a fairly vigorous climber, producing hanging clusters of pale yellow or creamy-white, velvety, nodding, bell-shaped flowers, with the bottom of each of the four petals curved upwards and backwards, reminding me of giant yellow bluebells.

The flowers are sweetly scented with a fragrance similar to that of cowslips.

This clematis should be pruned back hard each spring to a pair of strong buds 15–20 cm (6–8 in) above ground level.

ASPECT: Partial shade to full sun.
FLOWERING: July–October.
SCENT: Medium.
HARDINESS: -5 to -10 °C (23 to 14 °F).

3–6 m (10–20 ft)
2–3 m (7–10 ft)

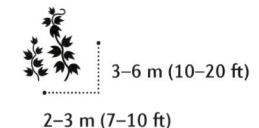

CLEMATIS TERNIFOLIA
Sweet autumn clematis
RANUNCULACEAE

The sweet autumn clematis is a vigorous, deciduous climber that will hold on to its leaves in mild winters, and as its common name suggests, it flowers late in the season.

The small, white, fragrant flowers are borne in large clusters, with cream-coloured anthers, and contrast well against the dark green foliage, which is divided into small leaflets on long stems.

The flowers are followed by fluffy seedheads.

Pruning should be carried out in late winter or early spring, cutting back hard to around 30 cm above ground level before new growth resumes.

ASPECT: Full sun to partial shade.
FLOWERING: August–November.
SCENT: Medium.
HARDINESS: -5 to -10 °C (23 to 14 °F).

3–5 m (10–16 ft)
2–3 m (7–10 ft)

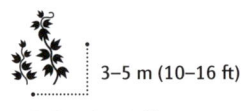

CLEMATIS × TRITERNATA
Clematis 'Rubromarginata'
RANUNCULACEAE

This is an attractive, deciduous clematis with relatively small flowers that are star-like and four-petalled. At the centre of the flowers the petals are white, edged and tipped with reddish-purple, and there is a showy boss of central stamens. The petals become almost reflexed as they age.

Clematis 'Rubromarginata' produces its almond-scented flowers in abundance and is a great climber when trained on a fence or arch, or when scrambling over a wall, where it will happily tolerate shade.

Pruning should be carried out in late winter or early spring, cutting back hard to around 30 cm above ground level before new growth resumes.

ASPECT: Full sun to partial shade.
FLOWERING: July–September.
SCENT: Light to strong.
HARDINESS: -5 to -10 °C (23 to 14 °F).

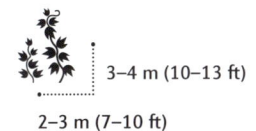

3–4 m (10–13 ft)
2–3 m (7–10 ft)

Clematis **'Rubromarginata'**

COCHLIASANTHUS CARACALLA
Snail vine
FABACEAE

If you want to try something a bit different and grow a plant that will be a talking point, then this very unusual-looking climber is worth a go.

Cochliasanthus caracalla may still be found under its former name of *Vigna caracalla*. It is most commonly called the snail vine but has another name, the corkscrew flower, which I think is more descriptive.

It is a vigorous climber with twining stems, so will need something like a trellis to attach itself to. The plant produces its extraordinary spiralling flowers – which are strongly fragrant and a mix of purple, creamish-white and sometimes pale orange – in hanging clusters of up to 20 individual blooms.

This is a tender plant and needs to be grown under glass, so it makes a good conservatory plant, where its delicious scent can be enjoyed.

Prune lightly after flowering to maintain its shape and size.

Cochliasanthus caracalla

ASPECT: Full sun to partial shade.
FLOWERING: July–September.
SCENT: Strong.
HARDINESS: Tender.

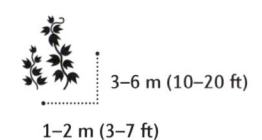

3–6 m (10–20 ft)
1–2 m (3–7 ft)

JASMINUM OFFICINALE
Common jasmine
OLEACEAE

The common jasmine is a highly scented, twining climber with clusters of 3–5 trumpet-like, star-shaped, pure white flowers that sometimes retain a pink tinge from their buds. Although it is deciduous, it will occasionally retain its ferny leaves if growing in a sheltered, frost-free area throughout the winter.

These dark green leaves are a perfect contrast to the white flowers, showing them off to their best effect. The cultivar **'Devon Cream'** has creamy-yellow flowers.

Jasminum officinale 'Devon Cream'

Jasminum officinale

Martin Leber / Alamy Stock Photo

There is also a variegated form, *Jasminum officinale* **'Aureum'**, with leaves that are blotched bright yellow, and equally fragrant flowers.

It is a fast-growing climber that needs some support for its twining stems to cling to, such as a trellis, or wires attached to fences or walls, and requires very little pruning apart from removing dead or damaged branches. Any pruning should be carried out straight after flowering.

ASPECT: Full sun to partial shade.
FLOWERING: June–August.
SCENT: Strong.
HARDINESS: -5 to -10 °C (23 to 14 °F).

3–6 m (10–20 ft)
1–2 m (3–7 ft)

LONICERA JAPONICA
Japanese honeysuckle
CAPRIFOLIACEAE

The Japanese honeysuckle is semi-evergreen with trumpet-like, tubular flowers borne in pairs. They are initially pure white and stand out well against its dark green foliage, but as the flowers mature and are pollinated, they turn a pretty pale yellow, and so throughout the summer there is always an attractive mix of both the white and yellow flowers. Most summers the flowers are followed by shiny black berries. It is best grown over a structure at a height where it can be controlled easily, as although this honeysuckle produces highly fragrant flowers, it comes with a word of caution: it is a very vigorous, twining climber that unless kept in check will quickly outgrow its space. Japanese honeysuckle is classed as a non-native, invasive plant in many countries. The plant is listed on Schedule 9 of the UK Wildlife & Countryside Act (Northern Ireland), making it an offence to plant or grow it in the wild in Northern Ireland.

That said, regular pruning by clipping over the whole plant in early spring, and if needed periodic cutting back hard to around 60 cm (2 ft) from the base, will keep it in check.
ASPECT: Partial shade to full sun.
FLOWERING: February–April.
SCENT: Strong.
HARDINESS: -5 to -10 °C (23 to 14 °F).

4–8 m (13–26 ft)
3–5 m (10–16 ft)

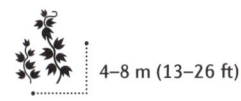

LONICERA PERICLYMENUM
Common honeysuckle
CAPRIFOLIACEAE

This pretty honeysuckle is native to the UK and parts of continental Europe. A deciduous, twining climber, it is often found growing naturally as a woodland plant and through road and trackside hedges. It makes a great addition to a wildlife garden as it is highly attractive to bees, butterflies, moths, and many other insects that are drawn in by its heady fragrance, particularly in the evenings. Its flowers are twin-lipped, creamy-white and yellow, often flushed reddish pink on their long, tubular bases, and have long, protruding, showy stamens. It's not quite as fragrant as the Japanese honeysuckle, but is not as rampant.

The cultivar **'Rhubarb and Custard'** is more reddish and yellow, whereas **'Graham Thomas'** has white flowers fading to yellow.

The flowers are produced on wood from the previous year, so pruning needs to be carried out immediately after flowering.
ASPECT: Partial shade to full sun.
FLOWERING: July–September.
SCENT: Medium.
HARDINESS: -5 to -10 °C (23 to 14 °F).

4–5 m (13–16 ft)
3–4 m (10–13 ft)

MANDEVILLA LAXA
Chilean jasmine
APOCYNACEAE

The Chilean jasmine is not a climber that is commonly grown. This may be because of its unreliable hardiness, though it has

Mandevilla laxa

happily survived several degrees of frost grown on a south-facing wall at Kew.

Its hardiness aside, it is a wonderfully vigorous plant, with large, shiny, semi-evergreen leaves (evergreen in its native South America), along long twining woody stems, producing large, white or creamy-white, funnel-shaped flowers that are strongly fragrant, particularly in the evening. It would be worth trying on a sheltered sunny wall or fence, or in cooler areas grown in a conservatory, where its fragrance would be better appreciated.

Any pruning is best carried out in late winter or early spring if grown indoors, or after the last frosts if grown outside, removing any damaged growths.
ASPECT: Full sun.
FLOWERING: July–September.
SCENT: Medium.
HARDINESS: 1 to 5 °C (34 to 41 °F).

3–4 m (10–13 ft)
1–2 m (3–7 ft)

Lonicera periclymenum

CLIMBERS

Roses

Like the shrub roses, climbing roses are a garden favourite, widening the choice of varieties and the way roses can be grown, particularly when it comes to adding height. They are ideal for growing over arches, pergolas, or trained along a fence or wall with some support.

There are two main types: climbing or rambling. As a general rule, the ramblers produce a mass of smallish flowers and flower only once a year, whereas the climbers often produce larger flowers which repeat flower (not always) throughout the summer.

Rosa **'Compassion'** is a climbing modern hybrid tea rose that produces wonderfully fragrant, apricot-pink flowers, repeating from June to October, 3 m x 2 m (10 x 6 ft). ***Rosa helenae*** is a species rambling type rose that has glaucous grey foliage and produces masses of clusters of single, creamy-white flowers with prominent yellow stamens,

Rosa **'Kew Rambler'**

Rosa **'Compassion'**

Rosa helenae

48 GARDENING WITH WINTER PLANTS

Rosa 'Rambling Rector'

Rosa 'Generous Gardener'

followed by attractive orange-red hips in autumn. Once-flowering in June–July. 6 m x 4.5 m (20 x 15 ft).

Rosa helenae is a species rambling type rose that has glaucous grey foliage and produces masses of clusters of single, creamy-white flowers with prominent yellow stamens, followed by attractive orange-red hips in autumn. Once-flowering in June–July. 6 m x 4.5 m (20 x 15 ft).

Rosa 'Kew Rambler' produces so many richly scented flowers that its glaucous foliage is almost completely hidden by them. They are borne in clusters of single, small, dark pink blooms that have white centres and golden yellow stamens. The flowers are followed by orange hips in autumn. Once-flowering in June–July. 6 m x 6 m (20 x 20 ft).

Rosa 'Paul's Himalayan Musk' has pale pink, double flowers, becoming white as they mature. It is a very free-flowering rose, with clusters of flowers borne in profusion, and a rampant climber. 7 m x 3 m (24 x 10 ft). Once-flowering June–July.

Rosa 'Rambling Rector' bears large clusters of creamy-white, semi-double flowers with attractive golden stamens when they first open, fading to brown as they mature. This is a very vigorous rose ideal for scrambling over large pergolas or summerhouses. The flowers are followed by red hips. Once-flowering in June–July. 7 m x 3 m (24 x 10 ft).

Rosa 'Shropshire Lass' is a tall climbing rose producing an abundance of large, semi-double, blush white flowers, opening from pink buds, and fading to white as they mature. This is a great rose for growing against a house wall with support. The flowers are followed by orange hips. Once-flowering in June–August. 4.5 m x 2 m (15 x 6 feet).

Rosa 'Generous Gardener' is an English climbing rose that bears beautiful pale pink double blooms with a good fragrance that is reminiscent of the old rose varieties. The arching stems are said to be thornless, but they always have a few, so beware. They repeat flower throughout the summer, from June to September. 4.5 m x 2 m (15 x 6 ft).

Any pruning that is needed to train rambling and climbing roses is best done in late winter or early spring.

ASPECT: Full sun or partial shade.
FLOWERING: June–September.
SCENT: Medium to strong.
HARDINESS: -5 to -10 °C (23 to 14 °F).

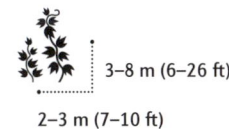

3–8 m (6–26 ft)
2–3 m (7–10 ft)

CLIMBERS 49

STAUNTONIA LATIFOLIA
Broad-leaved sausage vine
LARDIZABALACEAE

This climber has had a recent name change from *Holboellia latifolia*, and it is likely to be found under this previous name for some time to come.

The sausage vine is a very vigorous, evergreen climbing shrub with glossy, dark green leaves, which when young are tinged bronze. During spring it produces beautifully fragrant flowers with thick waxy petals, both male and female on the same plant. The male flowers are larger, green, and borne in small clusters, while the female flowers are smaller, generally in larger clusters, and purplish. Both male and female flowers are fragrant. The flowers are occasionally followed by purple, sausage-like fruits in autumn.

It is best trained against a wall or fence where its long twining stems can be tied in to supports, such as horizontal wires.

Regular pruning will be needed to keep this plant in check, and this should be carried out in spring after flowering, thinning some of the longer growths and removing any dead wood.

ASPECT: Full sun to partial shade.
FLOWERING: April–May.
SCENT: Strong.
HARDINESS: -1 to -5 °C (30 to 23 °F).

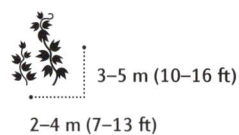

3–5 m (10–16 ft)
2–4 m (7–13 ft)

STAUNTONIA CORIACEA
Sausage vine
LARDIZABALACEAE

This climber is also commonly called the sausage vine and is very similar to *Stauntonia latifolia*, although it is hardier. Like *Stauntonia latifolia*, it is monoecious, having both male and female flowers on the same plant. However, the flowers are a lot smaller and creamy in colour, with many more female flowers than male. It has a similar strong fragrance and is equally vigorous with long, twining stems.

Regular pruning will be needed to keep this plant in check and should be carried out in spring after flowering, thinning some of the longer growths and removing any dead wood.

ASPECT: Full sun to partial shade.
FLOWERING: April–May.
SCENT: Strong.
HARDINESS: -5 to -10 °C (23 to 14 °F).

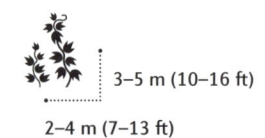

3–5 m (10–16 ft)
2–4 m (7–13 ft)

Stauntonia latifolia

Stauntonia coriacea

TRACHELOSPERMUM ASIATICUM
Asiatic jasmine
APOCYNACEAE

The Asiatic jasmine is a medium-sized, woody, evergreen climber, with glossy, dark green leaves. It produces wonderfully scented, star-like flowers during the summer months that are at first creamy-white, then pale yellow as they mature.

On a wall or fence, the long, twining stems need a support, such as a trellis or wires, to climb on and through. The evergreen foliage gives year-round interest and is the perfect background to the flowers.

The cultivar **'Pink Showers'** has soft pink flowers that are also beautifully fragrant and open a little earlier in May.

Flowers are produced on the previous year's growth, so any pruning and training should be carried out straight after flowering.

ASPECT: Full sun to partial shade.
FLOWERING: June–August.
SCENT: Medium.
HARDINESS: -5 to -10 °C (23 to 14 °F).

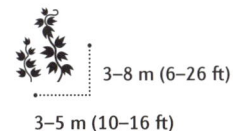

3–8 m (6–26 ft)
3–5 m (10–16 ft)

Trachelospermum asiaticum

TRACHELOSPERMUM JASMINOIDES
Star jasmine
APOCYNACEAE

Like the Asiatic jasmine, star jasmine is an evergreen woody climber that also needs a support system to enable it to climb. It is generally not as hardy as Asiatic jasmine and has larger leaves that will often turn reddish bronze in cold winters. It produces pure white, sweetly fragrant flowers in profusion that really stand out against the glossy leaves. Star jasmine is also more vigorous which makes it ideal for covering pergolas and archways. It will do best in a sunny sheltered spot out of cold winds.

Trachelospermum jasminoides

CLIMBERS 51

Trachelospermum jasminoides 'Variegatum'

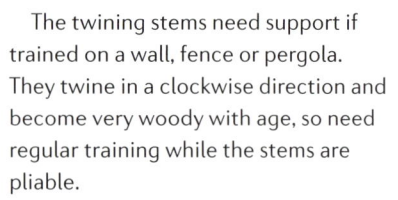

The twining stems need support if trained on a wall, fence or pergola. They twine in a clockwise direction and become very woody with age, so need regular training while the stems are pliable.

Both pink and white forms are available.

Pruning should be carried out in two stages with the intention of producing strong, spur-pruned laterals that will promote better flower-bud formation.

In mid-summer, the long trailing lateral growths should be cut back to a bud around 15 cm (6 in) from the main stems,

There is a variegated form, *Trachelospermum jasminoides* **'Variegatum'**, with creamy-white margins and blotches on the leaves, which are tinged reddish bronze in winter, adding to its year-round interest.

Flowers are produced on the previous year's growth so any pruning and training should be carried out straight after flowering.

ASPECT: Full sun to partial shade.
FLOWERING: June–August.
SCENT: Strong.
HARDINESS: -5 to -10 °C (23 to 14 °F).

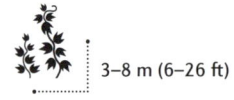

3–8 m (6–26 ft)
3–5 m (10–16 ft)

WISTERIA FLORIBUNDA
Japanese wisteria
FABACEAE

There can't be many people who would not put wisteria in their top three climbers. Their sheer flower power alone is enough to earn this ranking, but the fact that they are also scented is definitely a bonus. In late spring they are covered in large racemes of violet-blue, pea-like flowers gracefully hanging down 30 cm (12 in) or more, below the newly emerging leaves.

Wisteria floribunda 'Alba'

52 GARDENING WITH WINTER PLANTS

and then again in early to mid-winter to two buds from the main stems.
ASPECT: Full sun to partial shade.
FLOWERING: May–June.
SCENT: Medium.
HARDINESS: -5 to -10 °C (23 to 14 °F).

5–8 m (16–26 ft)
2–4 m (7–13 ft)

WISTERIA SINENSIS
Chinese wisteria

FABACEAE

Like the Japanese wisteria, the Chinese species is a large, deciduous climber, making it a striking plant that is often associated with cottage gardens, covering the walls of thatched dwellings. It is a vigorous climber with woody stems that twine in an anticlockwise direction. The fragrant flowers are lilac or mauve, opening just before the leaves, with racemes slightly shorter than those of the Japanese wisteria, around 15–20 cm (6–8 in).

Pruning wisterias should be carried out in two stages with the intention of producing strong, spur-pruned laterals that will promote better flower bud formation. In mid-summer, the long trailing lateral growths should be cut back to a bud around 15 cm (6 in) from the main stems, and then again in early to mid-winter, to two buds from the main stems.
ASPECT: Partial shade to full sun.
FLOWERING: May–June.
SCENT: Medium.
HARDINESS: -5 to -10 °C (23 to 14 °F).

3–8 m (6–26 ft)
2–4 m (7–13 ft)

Wisteria sinensis

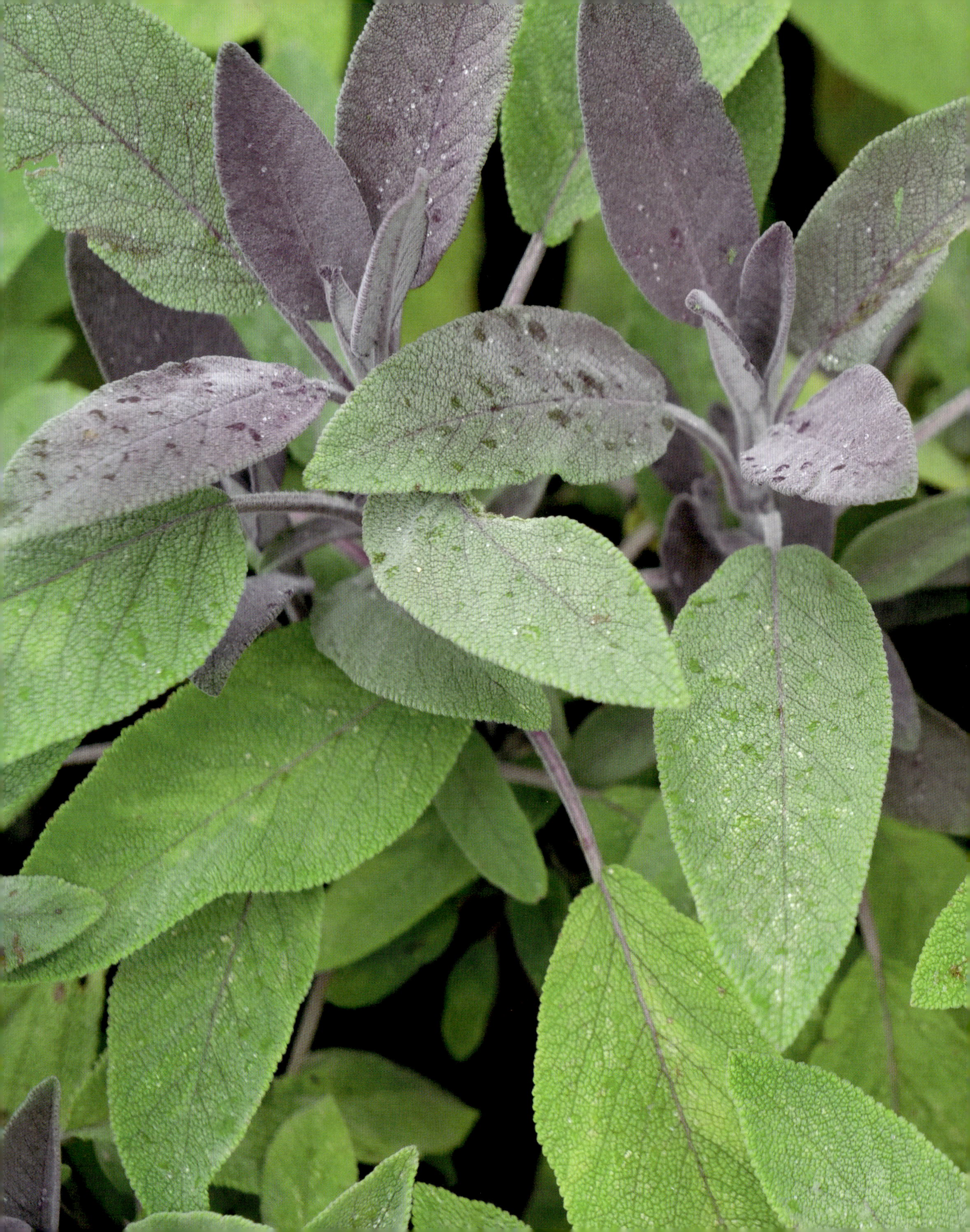

Herbs

ALLIUM SCHOENOPRASUM
Chives
AMARYLLIDACEAE

Chives have been used as an edible herb for millennia, but only cultivated in gardens since the 16th century. This is a hardy, bulbous perennial that produces long, cylindrical, hollow, pointed leaves with a mild onion scent when cut or crushed, and rounded purple flowerheads on inedible stems.

Chives do just as well grown in containers as they do in a bed or border, where they make an excellent edging plant in a mixed border. They are also used as a companion plant with roses to help prevent black spot. There is a saying, 'Chives next to roses create posies.'

Removing the flowerheads will increase leaf production. However, I find the flowering stems attractive, both to me and to pollinating insects, so I happily just leave them to flower, and I also use the flowerheads as an attractive addition to salads.

Every few years the clumps should be divided by lifting and reducing the number of bulbs in newly planted groups.

Remember that some leaves must be left to die back each year to strengthen the bulbs so that they can regenerate and produce leaves the following year.

ASPECT: Full sun or partial shade.
FLOWERING: May–July
SCENT: Light.
HARDINESS: -10 to -15 °C (14 to 5 °F).

25–30 cm (10–12 in)
5–10 cm (2–4 in)

ALOYSIA CITRODORA
Lemon verbena
VERBENACEAE

This small to medium-sized deciduous shrub is grown for its scented leaves, which are pale green, narrowly lance-shaped, and when rubbed or crushed release the most wonderfully strong scent of sweet lemons, reminding many people of lemon sherbet. In early summer it produces terminal panicles of small, white, or pale lilac flowers.

The scented leaves have many culinary uses as a flavouring, and are also used in potpourris and cosmetics.

Lemon verbena is not fully hardy, so in areas that get long and prolonged periods of frost it is best grown in a large container and moved to a frost-free location where it can be protected over winter.

Pruning should be carried out in spring once all chance of frost has passed and new growth has started, removing any dead tips. It can also be pruned quite hard to three or four buds to keep it small if grown in a container. New growth can be as late as early summer, so do not give up on it too early, thinking it's dead!

Aloysia citrodora

ASPECT: Full sun.
FLOWERING: July–August.
SCENT: Strong.
HARDINESS: 1 to -5 °C (34 to 23 °F).

1.5–2.5 m (5–8 ft)
1–2 m (3–7 ft)

ANETHUM GRAVEOLENS
Dill
APIACEAE

Dill is an annual herb so should be sown each year from fresh seed. The plants are rather fragile, particularly in wind, so are best given some support with a frame, or simply with twigs. If you are growing dill just for the leaves then several successional sowings should be made.

It is a very attractive plant with aromatic, feathery, fine green leaves and if left to flower will produce small clusters of tiny yellow flowers in a flattened umbel. Both flowers and seeds are edible.

Left in the ground the plants will self-seed, so they should be discarded at the

Allium schoenoprasum

Anethum graveolens

end of the season, unless you are happy for nature to take its course.
ASPECT: Full sun.
FLOWERING: July–October.
SCENT: Medium.
HARDINESS: 1 to -5 °C (34 to 23 °F).

60–150 cm (2–5 ft)
20–30 cm (8–12 in)

ANGELICA ARCHANGELICA
Angelica
APIACEAE

Angelica is a biennial, or short-lived perennial. Because of its height, it makes a great ornamental plant in the back of a border, where its stature can be appreciated.

It will produce a lot of leaves in its first year, but it is only in the plant's second year that it produces a large, sweetly scented, flowerhead, which consists of rounded umbels of small, greenish-white flowers.

Angelica archangelica

All parts of angelica are highly aromatic and the plant is commercially cultivated as an ingredient in cosmetics and medicines. Its young, candied stems are used as a decorative confectionery on cakes.

Angelica is fully hardy and will self-seed readily, producing new plants for successive flowering.
ASPECT: Full sun or partial shade.
FLOWERING: June–July.
SCENT: Strong.
HARDINESS: -10 to -15 °C (14 to 5 °F).

1–2.5 m (3–8 ft)
0.75–1 m (2½–3 ft)

ANTHRISCUS CEREFOLIUM
Chervil
APIACEAE

This aromatic herb is a hardy annual that has the flavour and scent of aniseed when its leaves are rubbed or bruised. It is one of the fines herbes used in French cooking, along with chives, tarragon and parsley, and is sometimes referred to as French parsley. Although a relative of parsley and very similar in looks, the aroma of its leaves is quite different, having a hint of aniseed.

The scented foliage is quite delicate and fern-like, with clusters of lacy, small white flowers in summer, which if left on the plant will self-seed. Being a hardy annual, it will survive over winter from late sowings, but for eating it is best kept under glass.
ASPECT: Full sun or partial shade.
FLOWERING: June to October
SCENT: Light.
HARDINESS: -10 to -15 °C (14 to 5 °F).

30–60 cm (1–2ft)
20–30 cm (10–12 in)

Anthriscus cerefolium

HERBS 57

ARTEMISIA DRACUNCULUS
Tarragon
ASTERACEAE

French tarragon is a half-hardy herbaceous perennial that is often referred to as the 'king of culinary herbs'. It is less hardy than the Russian variety, but its narrow, glossy leaves are more aromatic and have a sweeter, stronger aniseed flavour.

During summer, very small, almost insignificant yellow flowerheads are produced, but they very rarely set any viable seed. Because of this, cuttings should be taken from softwood tips in the summer to ensure you have plants for the following year, as without winter protection (at the minimum a mulch around the roots) the plant can't be guaranteed to survive. Alternatively, grow it in pots or containers that can be moved to a frost-free environment during the winter months.

ASPECT: Full sun.
FLOWERING: Insignificant, July–August
SCENT: Medium.
HARDINESS: Tender.

50–60 cm (20–24 in)
30–45 cm (12–18 in)

BORAGO OFFICINALIS
Borage
BORAGINACEAE

The showy, five-petalled flowers of borage are bright sky-blue and star-like with a darker central boss that is almost black, and dangle from upright stems. All parts of the plant's leaves and stems are covered in bristly hairs that give it an added attraction, and it is these that give off its wonderful, cucumber-like smell.

Borage is typically a cottage garden plant, lending itself to sunny mixed borders, and is great for attracting pollinating insects into the garden.

There is a white-flowered form, *Borago officinalis* 'Alba', and a variegated form, 'Bill Archer'.

The leaves and flowers of borage are edible and often used to add colour to salads, but its flowers are probably best known as a garnish for summer drinks.

The plant flowers all summer long, right up until the first frosts. Its seed can be collected, but it will readily self-seed each year.

ASPECT: Full sun or partial shade.
FLOWERING: June–September.
SCENT: Medium.
HARDINESS: -10 to -15 °C (14 to 5 °F).

50–60 cm (20–24 in)
30–50 cm (12–20 in)

Borago officinalis

Borago officinalis 'Alba'

Foeniculum vulgare

Foeniculum vulgare 'Giant Bronze'

FOENICULUM VULGARE
Fennel
APIACEAE

This is a very attractive perennial plant with fine, soft and feathery foliage, which has the aroma of aniseed when rubbed.

Its tall stature makes it an ideal plant for a mixed border, where it is mainly grown for its foliage, but during summer its tall stems are topped with an inflorescence made up of many small clusters (on long, arching stems) of tiny yellow flowers. It is drought-tolerant, working well in a gravel garden with other Mediterranean-type plants and grasses that enjoy similar growing conditions.

As well as looking good in an ornamental garden, fennel is great for herb gardens where the foliage, flowers and seeds – which all have an aniseed aroma and flavour – can be used to make tea, for cooking and in salads.

The cultivar **'Giant Bronze'**, with its bronze-purple foliage, will add a good colour contrast to a mixed border.
ASPECT: Full sun.
FLOWERING: July–August.
SCENT: Strong.
HARDINESS: -10 to -15 °C (14 to 5 °F).

1.5–2 cm (5–6½ ft)
30–45 cm (12–18 in)

HELICHRYSUM ITALICUM
Curry plant
ASTERACEAE

The curry plant is a small, bushy, evergreen sub-shrub with soft, silvery-grey, aromatic foliage that is strongly curry-scented and attractive all year round. During the summer, small clusters of flowers are produced on long stems sitting well above the foliage of the main plant, giving an overall domed effect.

Being native to Mediterranean regions means that the plant is very drought-tolerant once established and will grow well in a variety of positions, from containers to cottage gardens, gravel gardens, the front of a mixed border and grouped with other Mediterranean-type plants.

Pruning annually after flowering will improve flowering the following season and extend the life of the plant, preventing it from becoming too woody.
ASPECT: Full sun.
FLOWERING: June–September.
SCENT: Strong.
HARDINESS: -5 to -10 °C (23 to 14 °F).

20–50 cm (8–20 in)
30–75 cm (12–30 in)

Helichrysum italicum

HUMULUS LUPULUS
Hops
CANNABACEAE

Many herbs are commonly used in infusions to make teas, but the hops are used to make a very different drink and have been utilised for centuries in the beer-making industry.

This perennial climbing plant is a native of Britain and can be found growing naturally in many countryside hedgerows. It is dioecious, having male and female flowers on different plants.

As a cultivated plant it is a scrambling climber with long, twining stems that can be trained against a wall or fence, or over pergolas and arbours, where its scented, female, yellow-green flowers will mature into cone-like fruits that hang attractively in loose, showy clusters.

There is also a golden-leaved variety, *Humulus lupulus* **'Aureus'**, known as the golden hop, which will keep its colour best if grown in full sun.

Pruning should be carried out in late autumn, or it can be cut back close to the ground in winter from which it will sprout again in spring.

ASPECT: Full sun or partial shade.
FLOWERING: July–September.
SCENT: Medium.
HARDINESS: -10 to -15 °C (14 to 5 °F).

3–6 m (10–20 ft)
1.5–2 m (5–6½ ft)

HYSSOPUS OFFICINALIS
Hyssop
LAMIACEAE

Hyssop is a clump-forming, semi-evergreen, hardy perennial that has small, bright green, lance-shaped, aromatic leaves borne on tall, upright stems, and dense spikes of violet-blue or pink flowers with protruding stamens. There is also a white-flowered form available, *Hyssopus officinalis* f. *albus*.

The tubular flowers are particularly attractive to bees and other pollinating insects.

Hyssop grows very well as part of a mixed border, especially in drier, sunnier spots, as like most Mediterranean plants it is drought-tolerant.

It is grown commercially for its aromatic oil, which is distilled and used in flavourings. Both the leaves and flowers are edible.

Plants should be cut back hard in spring to avoid them becoming too woody.

ASPECT: Full sun.
FLOWERING: July–September.
SCENT: Medium.
HARDINESS: -10 to -15 °C (14 to 5 °F).

30–50 cm (12–20 in)
30–75 cm (12–30 in)

Humulus lupulus

Hyssopus officinalis

Laurus nobilis

LAURUS NOBILIS
Sweet bay
LAURACEAE

This is a very popular evergreen shrub or small tree that is suitable for lots of different situations in the garden. Its strongly aromatic leaves also have many culinary uses.

Bay produces masses of small, creamy-yellowish flowers in spring that are followed by small, glossy black berries, but this plant is really all about the foliage.

Its leathery, shiny mid-green leaves make this an attractive shrub all year round. If left to do its own thing, bay will grow to become quite tall, hence another of its common names: the bay tree. More commonly, it is grown as a hedge or trimmed and shaped as topiary. It grows well in a large container and of course is a must in any herb garden, where the aromatic leaves can be used either fresh or dried.

Regular pruning is needed to maintain this shrub at a manageable size and should be carried out in late winter or early spring, or more regularly if it is being topiarised.

ASPECT: Full sun or partial shade.
FLOWERING: May–June.
SCENT: Strong.
HARDINESS: -10 to -15 °C (14 to 5 °F).

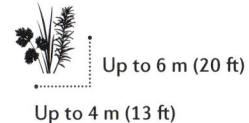

Up to 6 m (20 ft)
Up to 4 m (13 ft)

LEVISTICUM OFFICINALE
Lovage
APIACEAE

Lovage, which is the sole species within the genus *Levisticum*, is a tall perennial with hairless, celery-scented leaves.

During the summer, flat clusters of small, greenish-yellow flowers are produced and followed by edible seeds that have the same strong celery taste and aroma. The Ancient Greeks grew lovage as a medicinal herb to aid digestion.

Like many herbaceous plants, lovage should be cut back in the autumn.

ASPECT: Full sun.
FLOWERING: July–August.
SCENT: Medium.
HARDINESS: -10 to -15 °C (14 to 5 °F).

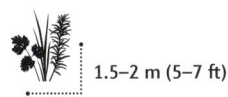

1.5–2 m (5–7 ft)
30–75 cm (12–30 in)

Levisticum officinale

HERBS 61

Matricaria chamomilla

MATRICARIA CHAMOMILLA
Scented mayweed
ASTERACEAE

Scented mayweed is an annual plant that is native to southern Europe and was originally introduced into Britain with the spread of agriculture. It's a plant that looks very similar to corn camomile, which was also introduced at around the same time.

It has a daisy-like flower with feathery, finely divided leaves that when crushed have a strong aromatic scent. The flowers are also scented and borne singly in clusters on long terminal stems.

Like most cornfield annuals it will self-seed, but regular ground disturbance is needed for it to germinate and it is often outcompeted by perennials.

ASPECT: Full sun or partial shade.
FLOWERING: June to August.
SCENT: Medium.
HARDINESS: -10 to -15 °C (14 to 5 °F).

20–50 cm (8–20 in)
20–50 cm (8–20 in)

MELISSA OFFICINALIS
Lemon balm
LAMIACEAE

Lemon balm is a tough, bushy, herbaceous perennial that is grown for its aromatic foliage. It has been cultivated since at least the 16th century.

When rubbed, the coarse, mid-green leaves produce a lovely mild lemon aroma. They are used as a herb in teas (one, known as melissa tea, is said to promote sleep) and as a flavouring. The oil extract is also used in perfumery.

During summer, small white flowers are borne in rounded clusters from the leaf axils. The flowers are rich in nectar, making this an excellent bee plant.

Lemon balm can become a bit of a thug, spreading by underground roots and seeding in a similar way to mint, so cutting it back after flowering and restricting it by growing it in a container are advisable.

ASPECT: Full sun or partial shade.
FLOWERING: June–August.
SCENT: Medium.
HARDINESS: -10 to -15 °C (14 to 5 °F).

30–60 cm (1–2 ft)
30–75 cm (12–30 in)

Melissa officinalis

MENTHA × PIPERITA
Peppermint
LAMIACEAE

There are many different and interesting mints, from the most common garden mint, *Mentha spicata*, to banana- (*Mentha arvensis* 'Banana'), chocolate- (*Mentha × piperita* f. *citrata* 'Chocolate') and grapefruit-scented (*Mentha × piperita* f. *citrata* 'Grapefruit').

Peppermint is a hybrid between two other mints, spearmint and watermint, and is said to be the mint with the strongest flavour.

It has bright green leaves and upright, purple stems. As they grow, the stems become lax and root readily where they touch the ground, so peppermint can be very quick to spread. It produces pale purple flowering spikes in mid-summer that attract many different pollinators.

All mints are perennial, regrowing each year, and most are particularly vigorous so are best grown in containers to restrict their growth and to avoid them spreading through beds and borders.

Mentha × piperita

After flowering, cut plants back to around 5 cm (2 in) above ground level.
ASPECT: Full sun or partial shade.
FLOWERING: July–August.
SCENT: Strong.
HARDINESS: -10 to -15 °C (14 to 5 °F).

30–60 cm (1–2 ft)
60–150 cm (2–5 ft)

MONARDA DIDYMA
Bergamot
LAMIACEAE

Bergamot not only has its culinary uses, it also makes a great herbaceous plant for a mixed border, where its distinctive, showy flowers stand out well against the aromatic, mid-green leaves, which have a minty fragrance. In addition, the flowers are extremely attractive to bees and butterflies.

The large, scarlet-red inflorescences are produced in dense terminal whorls above dark red bracts. They are made up of many individual, two-lipped tubular flowers, and in their native North America are visited by hummingbirds and other pollinators.

Cut back this herbaceous perennial in late autumn after flowering has finished, and divide congested clumps every few years.
ASPECT: Full sun or partial shade.
FLOWERING: June–August.
SCENT: Strong.
HARDINESS: -10 to -15 °C (14 to 5 °F).

60–90 cm (2–3 ft)
30–45 cm (12–18 in)

OCIMUM BASILICUM
Sweet basil
LAMIACEAE

Basil is a tender, half-hardy annual when grown outdoors but can be grown as a short-lived perennial if given winter protection in a glasshouse.

The bright green, tender leaves produce a wonderful aroma when crushed. It will bear clusters of small, white, tubular flowers arranged in whorls during summer, but these should be pinched out to keep the basil producing new leaves.

This is a herb long associated with tomatoes in salads. It is also a good companion plant to grow with tomatoes as it deters whitefly.

There are other varieties, for example the purple-leaved form, as well as cinnamon, lemon, and lime basils.
ASPECT: Full sun or partial shade.
FLOWERING: June–August.
SCENT: Strong.
HARDINESS: -10 to -15 °C (14 to 5 °F).

30–45 cm (12–18 in)
20–30 cm (10–12 in)

Monarda didyma

Ocimum basilicum

Origanum vulgare

ORIGANUM VULGARE
Oregano
LAMIACEAE

Oregano is a very pretty and popular herb that is native to Britain. During the summer months, small, mounded clumps can be found growing in short grassland areas on chalky soils, covered in small pink or purple flowers that attract both bees and butterflies.

Confusingly, it is also known as wild marjoram in Britain, but while the closely related and equally aromatic marjoram, *Origanum majorana*, is very similar, it produces white flowers and is native to Cyprus and Turkey.

In cultivation in richer soils, the plants grow taller from their woody base and have larger leaves, and the flowers are a bit more variable in colour: mauve, pale pink or white.

Cut back plants in late summer by around half, which will prevent them from becoming too woody and straggly.

ASPECT: Full sun.
FLOWERING: July–September.
SCENT: Medium.
HARDINESS: -10 to -15 °C (14 to 5 °F).

20–30 cm (10–12 in)
30–45 cm (12–18 in)

SALVIA ROSMARINUS
Rosemary
LAMIACEAE

Until 2017, the Latin name for rosemary was *Rosmarinus officinalis* and it will probably still be found under that name for some time to come. What hasn't changed is the aromatic oils within this 'wonder herb' that make it so popular.

Rosemary is a very versatile, small to medium-sized evergreen shrub with small, thick, linear aromatic leaves, and flowers that range in colour from white to pinks and mauves, produced over a very long period. As well as growing in a herb garden, rosemary will do very well in a large pot or container on a sunny patio, in a mixed border, or cottage garden.

It is very drought-tolerant once established. In common with many such plants from the Mediterannean region, it has small leaves with their inrolled margins, which reduce the amount of moisture lost.

Its young leaves are the most aromatic and are used in a variety of culinary ways, from flavouring bread and meat, to infusing for herbal tea.

'Rosea' is a pink-flowered cultivar. **'Miss Jessopp's Upright'** is an upright cultivar that will grow to 1.5 m tall.

Annual pruning should be carried out after flowering to keep plants healthy, but avoid cutting back into old wood, as they do not respond well to heavy pruning.

ASPECT: Full sun.
FLOWERING: April–December.
SCENT: Strong.
HARDINESS: 0 to -5 °C (32 to 23 °F).

60–150 cm (2–5 ft)
60–150 cm (2–5 ft)

Salvia rosmarinus

SALVIA VULGARIS
Common sage
LAMIACEAE
This is an evergreen, bushy sub-shrub with highly aromatic, softly hairy, glaucous leaves, and stems covered with downy hairs to give a whitish silvery appearance. These characteristics make common sage a valuable decorative plant in an ornamental border, adding contrasting texture and colour.

During the summer, upright flower spikes are produced with lavender-coloured, two-lipped flowers that are also scented.

Sage is a herb that has been grown for centuries. Its old Latin name, *salveo*, means to heal, and it is still used today as a remedy for sore throats and coughs.

ASPECT: Full sun.
FLOWERING: June–August.
SCENT: Strong.
HARDINESS: -10 to -15 °C (14 to 5 °F).

30–60 cm (1–2 ft)
60–90 cm (2–3 ft)

Salvia vulgaris

Tanacetum parthenium

TANACETUM PARTHENIUM
Feverfew
ASTERACEAE
This is a hardy and vigorous herbaceous perennial with very attractive, small, daisy-like flowers that are produced from mid to late summer, attracting many beneficial insects to the garden. They make excellent cut flowers that can be used fresh or dried for long-lasting arrangements and potpourri.

The lacy leaves of feverfew are highly aromatic, and its tall, branched stems form rounded clumps covered with the fern-like, finely divided foliage, which can be used as a natural repellent to ants, flies and wasps in the house.

It will readily self-seed. Seedheads can be snipped off to prevent its spread, although unwanted seedlings are easily removed.

Medicinally it is used to treat migraines and reduce fevers.

ASPECT: Full sun or partial shade.
FLOWERING: July–September.
SCENT: Medium.
HARDINESS: -10 to -15 °C (14 to 5 °F).

50–60 cm (20–24 in)
20–30 cm (10–12 in)

TANACETUM VULGARE
Tansy
ASTERACEAE
This tall perennial, also known as golden buttons, has handsome dark green, aromatic, fern-like foliage, with each of its leaves divided into many finely toothed leaflets. It has a long history of medicinal use.

The plant produces eye-catching, flat-topped, terminal clusters of yellow, button-like flowers that are lightly scented and very attractive to many

Tanacetum vulgare

Tanacetum vulgare

Thymus × citriodorus

pollinators, but it also deters many unwanted pests with the release of a strong camphor-like scent when the leaves are crushed.

Tansy does have a habit of spreading quickly in ideal conditions, both by seed and underground rhizomes, so it might need to be regularly kept in check.

Bunches cut and kept as dried flowers, as well as being attractive, are said to deter flies in the home. In centuries past, the leaves were finely shredded and added to flat cakes called tansies that were eaten during Lent.
ASPECT: Full sun.
FLOWERING: June–September.
SCENT: Medium.
HARDINESS: -10 to -15 °C (14 to 5 °F).

0.6–1 m (2–3 ft)

50–60 cm (20–24 in)

THYMUS × CITRIODORUS
Lemon thyme
LAMIACEAE

This wonderful little lemon-scented, evergreen sub-shrub is a natural hybrid between *Thymus pulegioides* and *Thymus vulgaris*, which both occur in France and Spain.

It produces a small and compact bushy plant with small, diamond-shaped leaves that carry its delightful scent. In summer, lemon thyme is covered with clusters of small, attractive mauve or pink flowers.

Its low-spreading habit makes it an ideal groundcover plant for a gravel garden, for the front of a border, or as a container-grown herb.

Regular trimming will keep the plant supplying its fresh edible leaves and flowers.
ASPECT: Full sun.
FLOWERING: June–August.
SCENT: Medium.
HARDINESS: -10 to -15 °C (14 to 5 °F).

30–45 cm (12–18 in)

30–50 cm (12–20 in)

THYMUS VULGARIS
Common thyme
LAMIACEAE

This dwarf evergreen sub-shrub is a very popular culinary herb. Its small, oval, dark green leaves are aromatic and produce a low, rounded, dense and bushy plant that in late spring and early summer is topped with tiny pink flowers, which are a magnet for bees.

Its small size makes it ideal for growing in pots or as an edging plant along a sunny border in a cottage or gravel garden, where it will release its scent as you brush past it.

Keep regularly cutting and trimming the plant to encourage new growth and prevent it becoming too woody.
ASPECT: Full sun.
FLOWERING: May–July.
SCENT: Medium.
HARDINESS: -10 to -15 °C (14 to 5 °F).

20–30 cm (10–12 in)

20–30 cm (10–12 in)

OPPOSITE
Thymus vulgaris

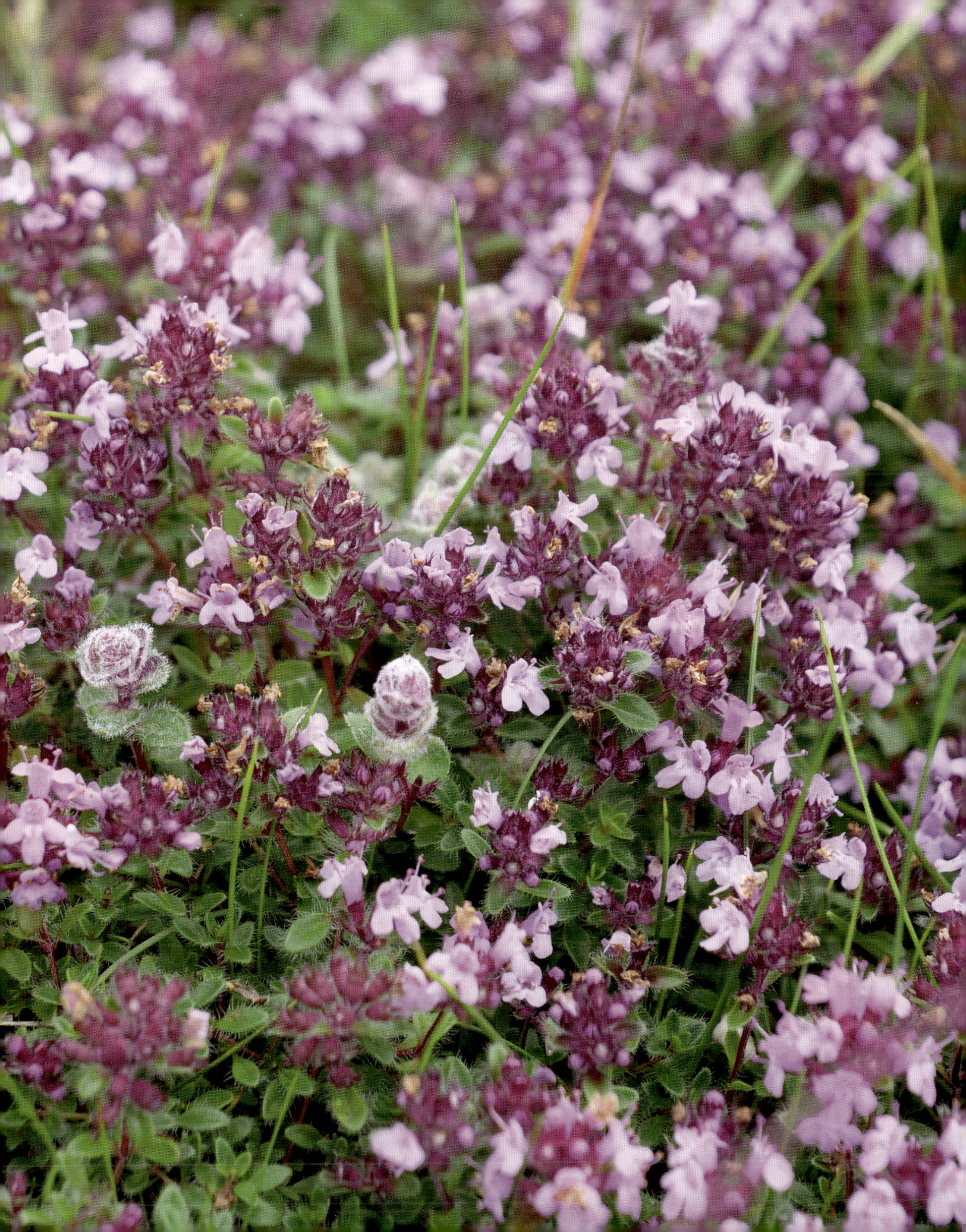

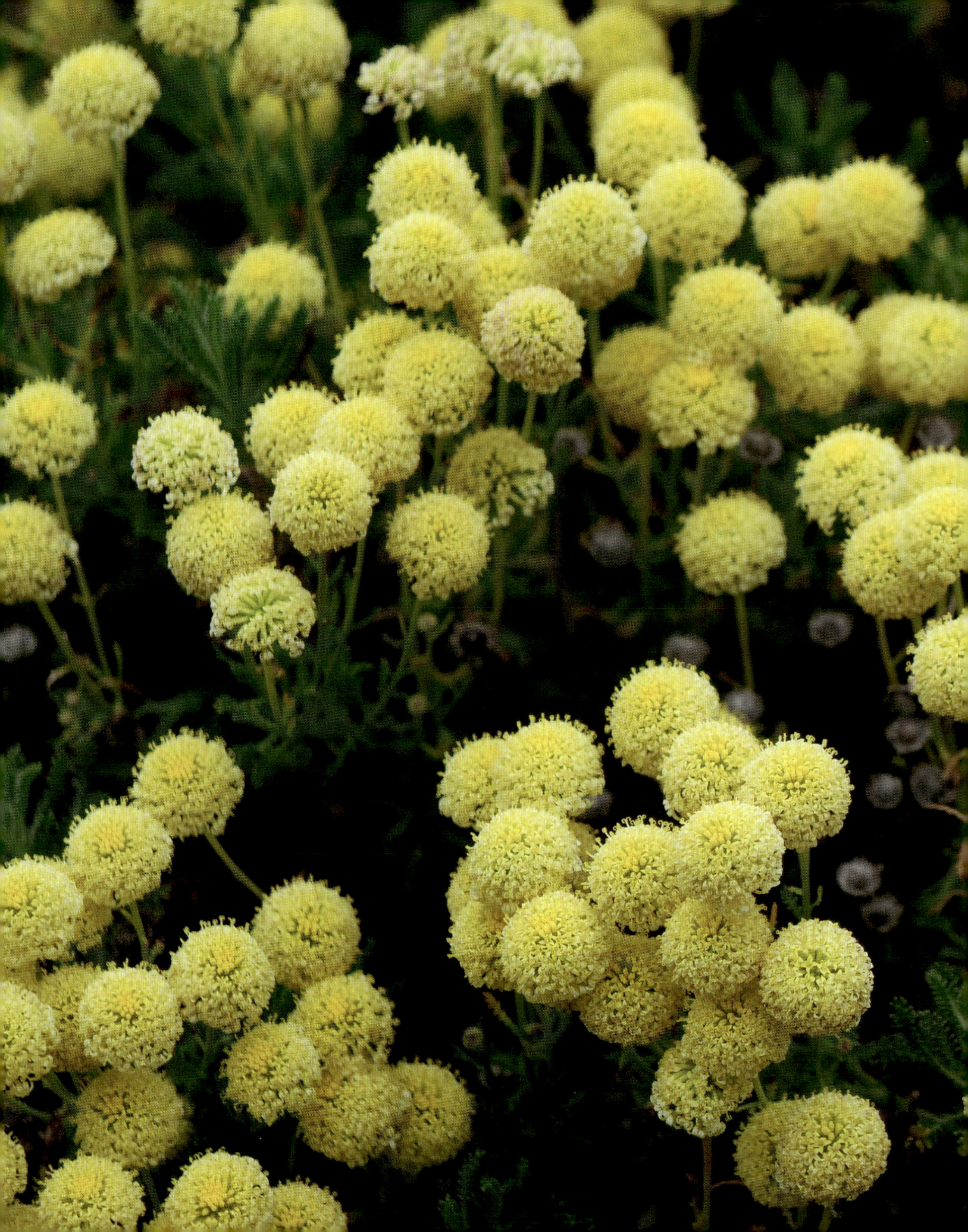

attractive bushy clump and is drought-tolerant once established.

During the summer months it will produce tiny, almost insignificant yellow flowers, but they form terminal sprays that can be quite showy.

The aromatic foliage is a well-known ingredient in the alcoholic drink absinthe.

Although this perennial does deter some unwanted insects from your borders, it also has the annoying habit of attracting aphids.

ASPECT: Full sun or partial shade.
FLOWERING: July–August.
SCENT: Medium.
HARDINESS: -10 to -15 °C (14 to 5 °F).

60–90 cm (24–36 in)
45–60 cm (18–24 in)

CLINOPODIUM NEPETA
Lesser calamint
LAMIACEAE

Until recently, this aromatic perennial plant was known as *Calamintha nepeta* but has undergone a name change. I am sure it will be found under its old name for some time to come.

Lesser calamint produces a compact, bushy plant, which from mid- to late summer is loosely covered in pale lilac, tubular flowers right up until the first frosts. It is highly attractive to bees, which enjoy the nectar-rich flowers continually all summer. It is also drought tolerant.

It is the grey-green foliage that produces the fragrance from this plant. Crushing or brushing against its leaves releases a minty-lemon fragrance, so it is best planted close to the front of a bed or border where it will sprawl over the edges.

There is a white-flowered cultivar called **'White Cloud'**.

Cut back plants after flowering to keep them compact and tidy, and to help it reflower.

Clinopodium nepeta

ASPECT: Full sun or partial shade.
FLOWERING: July–September.
SCENT: Medium.
HARDINESS: -10 to -15 °C (14 to 5 °F).

50–60 cm (20–24 in)
30–50 cm (12–20 in)

COSMOS ATROSANGUINEUS
Chocolate cosmos
ASTERACEAE

Although not fully hardy, this plant is worth growing for its scent alone. It will survive most winters and will fit into many garden situations, from cottage gardens to modern mixed borders, as well as making an excellent cut flower.

Chocolate cosmos is best grown in a hot, sunny border where its velvety, brownish-red flowers – each borne singly on tall stems – can show themselves off to their best effect and produce the richest chocolatey and vanilla scents.

Regular deadheading will encourage longer flowering.

The tubers can be lifted and stored over winter in a frost-free place. Alternatively, like dahlias they can be protected with a thick covering of mulch.

ASPECT: Full sun or partial shade.
FLOWERING: June–September.
SCENT: Medium.
HARDINESS: 1 to -5 °C (33 to 23 °F).

50–75 cm (20 in–2.5 ft)
30–45 cm (12–18 in)

Cosmos atrosanguineus

DIANTHUS BARBATUS
Sweet William
CARYOPHYLLACEAE

Many of the plants referred to as cottage garden plants are perennials that are scented, and sweet William is a wonderful scented plant and one that has been a favourite as a cottage garden plant for centuries. It produces flattened clusters of sweetly scented flowers on tall, erect stems in varying colours, mainly single pinks and reds, but also bicolour and double-flowered forms.

Sweet William is a short-lived perennial but is often grown as a biennial, with fresh seed sown each year. But plants will survive for a few years in most conditions, and they will also self-seed.

It makes a great plant for the front of a border, in mixed plantings and as a container plant.

Deadhead regularly to extend the flowering period, which should continue right up until the first frosts.

ASPECT: Full sun or partial shade.
FLOWERING: June–September.
SCENT: Strong.
HARDINESS: -10 to -15 °C (14 to 5 °F).

30–45 cm (12–18 in)
25–30 cm (10–12 in)

DIANTHUS CARYOPHYLLUS
Carnation
CARYOPHYLLACEAE

Most of the carnations grown today are cultivars that come in a range of colours but retain their sweet, clove-like fragrance.

They are also known as pinks due to their 'pinked' petal edges. Stiff, erect stems, which grow from a low cluster of glaucous leaves, bear the multi-petalled blooms.

Carnations are perfect for a sunny border, and their tall stems make them a

Dianthus caryophyllus

good cut flower, adding fragrance to a bouquet.

Deadhead them regularly to ensure continual flowering. Dividing the clumps every few years will keep them healthy and maintain their vigour.

ASPECT: Full sun or partial shade.
FLOWERING: June–September.
SCENT: Strong.
HARDINESS: -10 to -15 °C (14 to 5 °F).

40–60 cm (16–24 in)
25–30 cm (10–12 in)

DISPOROPSIS PERNYI
Evergreen Solomon's seal
ASPARAGACEAE

This is an unusual, clump-forming evergreen perennial that is best grown in semi-shade as it is a woodland plant from the mountain forests of China.

It produces dark green, arching, leafy stems, which are speckled with brown blotches when young. The small, creamy-

Disporopsis pernyi

white, bell-shaped flowers with reflexed tips are greenish inside and have a delicate, lemony scent. They droop beneath the leaves from the leaf axils. The flowers are followed by dark purple berries.

This perennial will slowly develop into small clumps that will benefit from having the older stems removed to allow the newer, more colourful stems to develop.

ASPECT: Partial shade.
FLOWERING: April–June.
SCENT: Light.
HARDINESS: -10 to -15 °C (14 to 5 °F).

50–60 cm (20–24 in)
30–50 cm (12–20 in)

FILIPENDULA ULMARIA
Meadowsweet
ROSACEAE

Meadowsweet is a tall, upright perennial found naturally growing in damp soils, often close to streams and rivers, making it an ideal plant for growing in soil that is regularly damp and moisture-retentive. The margins of a pond would suit it well, but it will not tolerate the roots being totally submerged for any length of time.

It is a plant often grown just for its attractive ferny foliage, but its small, fragrant, creamy-white flowers are a delight, each one filled with protruding stamens. The large, frothy, terminal clusters of flowers have an almond fragrance that fills the air on still summer days.

Once flowering has finished, the stems can be cut back to ground level or left to self-seed and cut back later in the year.
ASPECT: Full sun or partial shade.
FLOWERING: June–August.
SCENT: Strong.
HARDINESS: -10 to -15 °C (14 to 5 °F).

0.6–1 m (2–3 ft)
30–45 cm (12–18 in)

Filipendula ulmaria

Galium odoratum

GALIUM ODORATUM
Sweet woodruff

RUBIACEAE

Sweet woodruff is a deciduous plant that is a native of British woodlands and so makes a good low-growing plant for ground cover in shady areas under and around trees. It spreads via creeping rhizomes. Once established, it is also drought-tolerant so can even survive dry shade.

The clusters of dainty white, star-like flowers are held above the bright green leaves that grow in whorls along their stems.

If sweet woodruff outgrows its space (although it is fairly well behaved) it can be lifted and divided or simply thinned out in late autumn or early spring.

The scent of the flowers and leaves intensifies when dried and so they are often used in potpourri.
ASPECT: Partial shade.
FLOWERING: April–July.
SCENT: Light.
HARDINESS: -10 to -15 °C (14 to 5 °F).

15–30 cm (6–12 in)
0.5–1 m (1.5–3 ft)

PERENNIALS

GERANIUM MACRORRHIZUM
Big-root cranesbill
GERANIACEAE

This geranium is semi-evergreen with large, rounded leaves that are divided into small lobed sections.

The pinkish flowers have long, protruding, showy stamens. They are quite small but are held high above the foliage on tall stems that stand out well against the carpeting foliage, which is strongly fragrant and in most years gives good, reddish autumn colour.

Big-root cranesbill is a plant that will tolerate full shade and is drought tolerant, so ideal for ground cover in a difficult shady corner, where it will supress weeds and hide the leaves of earlier flowering bulbs as they die back.

There is also a white-flowered variety named **'White Ness'** and a paler pink **'Ingwersen's Variety'**.

ASPECT: Partial shade or full sun.
FLOWERING: May–September.
SCENT: Medium.
HARDINESS: -10 to -15 °C (14 to 5 °F).

30–50 cm (12–20 in)
40–60 cm (16–24 in)

HESPERIS MATRONALIS
Sweet rocket
BRASSICACEAE

Although classed as a short-lived perennial, sweet rocket is often grown as a biennial. But it will freely self-seed, so will reappear in your garden year after year. In many ways it is similar in looks to annual honesty, *Lunaria annua*.

The four-petalled flowers of sweet rocket vary in colour from deep purples through to white, but most commonly lilac. It will grow well in a mixed border and is a great beneficial plant for wildlife, spreading and naturalising by seed in the wilder parts of a garden and eventually making quite large, bushy plants.

Like many scented plants, the fragrance is most noticeable on warm, still evenings.

Deadheading will extend the flowering period, but make sure some flowers are left to set seed to continue providing new plants.

ASPECT: Full sun or partial shade.
FLOWERING: May–July.
SCENT: Medium.
HARDINESS: -10 to -15 °C (14 to 5 °F).

0.6–1 m (2–3 ft)
30–45 cm (12–18 in)

Geranium macrorrhizum

Hesperis matronalis

GARDENING WITH SCENTED PLANTS

LUNARIA REDIVIVA
Perennial honesty
BRASSICACEAE

While it is not as commonly grown as the annual honesty, this has a longer season, flowering from late spring well into summer. The flowers are lilac to pale pink, produced in terminal clusters on upright stems, with bright green, heart-shaped leaves, forming tight clumps.

The attractive silvery, translucent, paper-like seedheads produced after flowering in early autumn are oval with a tapering, pointed tip (those of annual honesty are rounded), and make an attractive feature if left after flowering. They are also useful in dried flower arrangements.

Perennial honesty works well in borders, cottage-style gardens and naturalised in woodlands.

ASPECT: Full sun or partial shade.
FLOWERING: May–August.
SCENT: Medium.
HARDINESS: -10 to -15 °C (14 to 5 °F).

0.6–1 cm (2–3 ft)
20–30 cm (8–12 in)

MATTHIOLA INCANA
Brompton stocks
BRASSICACEAE

This is a traditional cottage garden perennial with a tall, dense spike of clove-scented flowers that come in a range of colours.

It's also commonly known as the hoary stock due to its glaucous, lance-shaped leaves being covered in fine hairs, giving them a 'hoary' appearance.

The flowers are borne in clusters along a tall flowering spike and produce a sweet, spicy fragrance. Pinching out the tips of the plants will encourage them to produce side branches and more flowers.

Lunaria rediviva

Brompton stocks will grow well in a container as well as in mixed herbaceous borders and they make excellent cut flowers.

ASPECT: Full sun or partial shade.
FLOWERING: June–August.
SCENT: Medium.
HARDINESS: -10 to -15 °C (14 to 5 °F).

50–60 cm (20–24 in)
30–50 cm (12–20 in)

MYRRHIS ODORATA
Sweet cicely
APIACEAE

This is a very attractive herbaceous plant that in some cases can reach 2 metres tall, though usually a little less. Its stems are soft and hairy and it has distinctive, fern-like foliage, giving the whole plant an open and airy appearance. Its tiny white flowers are borne in small, branched umbels.

The leaves are used as a herb for flavouring and have a sweet aniseed scent when crushed. Its roots and seeds are also edible, making it an ideal plant for a herb garden, but it looks great in a mixed herbaceous border, adding height and stature.

As clumps spread they can be divided in autumn or left to self-seed, naturally enhancing the edges of a shady woodland garden.

ASPECT: Partial shade to full sun.
FLOWERING: May–July.
SCENT: Medium.
HARDINESS: -10 to -15 °C (14 to 5 °F).

0.75–1.5 m (2.5–5 ft)
0.5–1 m (1.5–3 ft)

NEPETA CATARIA
Catmint
LAMIACEAE

This is a perennial plant that is similar in many ways to the lesser catmint *Clinopodium nepeta*, with its aromatic foliage, but has a more upright growth habit, with branched stems that carry long terminal spikes of small white or lilac flowers with purple spots. Like those of the lesser catmint, these are very attractive to butterflies, bumblebees, honeybees, and solitary bees.

The aromatic leaves are loved by cats, due to the presence of a chemical called nepetalactone. The chemical evolved as an insect repellent to prevent attacks from herbivorous insects, but cats just love it, rolling in the plant and rubbing their heads and bodies in it. It has this effect whether growing or dried.

Cut back plants after flowering to keep them compact and tidy – especially after any cats have enjoyed it!

ASPECT: Full sun.
FLOWERING: June–September.
SCENT: Medium.
HARDINESS: -10 to -15 °C (14 to 5 °F).

50–60 cm (20–24 in)
30–50 cm (12–20 in)

PAEONIA LACTIFLORA
Chinese peony
PAEONIACEAE

Although the straight species is available, the most commonly grown Chinese peonies are cultivars and there are quite a few to choose from. They make a great addition to a mixed border in late spring and early summer.

Herbaceous peonies start to push up through the ground in early spring and quickly develop into a rounded, bushy mound of dark green leaves.

The flowers are particularly large and showy, and both the original Chinese peony and its cultivars are fragrant.

Paeonia lactiflora 'Dinner Plate' is a large (as a dinner plate) pink-flowered cultivar with the centre of the flower filled with smaller petals.

Paeonia lactiflora 'Félix Crousse' has heavily scented, magenta flowers, with finely cut leaves.

Paeonia lactiflora 'Sarah Bernhardt', like all of these cultivars, bears enormous, showy flowers. They are rose-pink with paler white edges, and fully double.

These herbaceous peonies often need their stems supporting because the large flowerheads are particularly heavy.

Nepeta cataria

Paeonia lactiflora

As well as looking good in the garden, they all make good cut flowers and should be cut in the bud once they show colour.
ASPECT: Full sun.
FLOWERING: June–July.
SCENT: Medium.
HARDINESS: -10 to -15 °C (14 to 5 °F).

50–75 cm (20–30 in)
50–75 cm (20–30 in)

PETASITES PYRENAICUS
Winter heliotrope
ASTERACEAE

Until recently also known a *Petasites fragrans*, this creeping perennial has large, rounded leaves that give the genus its name, from the Greek *petasos*, a broad-brimmed hat with a similar shape. The leaves appear after the pale lilac-mauve inflorescences, which are borne on tall, loose spikes, with tiny clusters of individual flowers that have a vanilla fragrance, which some say reminds them of cherry pie.

This is probably not a plant for growing in a normal garden situation unless you have a wild area where it can be left to spread naturally, quickly forming a carpet of ground cover that will survive in relatively dry soils. But winter heliotrope will also do well grown in a large container, which is how it first arrived in Britain from its native Italy in the 19th century.
ASPECT: Full sun.
FLOWERING: December–March.
SCENT: Medium.
HARDINESS: -10 to -15 °C (14 to 5 °F).

15–20 cm (6–8 in)
1–1.5 m (3–5 ft)

PHLOX DIVARICATA
Wild sweet William
POLEMONIACEAE

This native of North America is a semi-evergreen perennial that grows in clearings and on the edges of woodland, where it is also known as the woodland phlox, so is best suited to similar growing environments in our gardens. But it is also suitable for wildlife gardens as it is a very good source of both nectar and pollen. It will tolerate being in a border that is sunny for part of the day.

The fragrant flowers are lavender-blue and produced in loose terminal clusters over a long period in late spring and early summer.

Clumps will slowly increase from their mat-forming, creeping rhizomes. Deadheading will extend flowering but is a bit tricky with the smallish flowers.
ASPECT: Partial shade.
FLOWERING: May–June.
SCENT: Medium.
HARDINESS: -10 to -15 °C (14 to 5 °F).

25–50 cm (10–20 in)
30–50 cm (12–20 in)

PHLOX PANICULATA
Perennial phlox
POLEMONIACEAE

Like so many of the scented perennials, this is a classic plant of cottage gardens.

The tall and erect stems have narrow, dark green foliage, which contrasts well with the colours of the flowers, which are most commonly pinks and purples, although white and blue varieties are available.

Because of its height it works well both at the back of a border or mixed in throughout a border. The long-lasting blooms will fit in well with most colour schemes and the stiff stems rarely need staking. However, it does need to be kept moist at the roots, as it will suffer in dry, hot conditions.

It is a very long-lasting perennial and dividing it every few years will keep it growing healthily.
ASPECT: Full sun or partial shade.
FLOWERING: June–September.
SCENT: Medium.
HARDINESS: -10 to -15 °C (14 to 5 °F).

1–1.5 m (3–5 ft)
0.5–1 m (1½–3 ft)

Phlox paniculata 'Fuji'

PRIMULA VERIS
Cowslip
PRIMULACEAE

It's such a pretty sight to see a meadow in early spring filled with this wonderful flower, which is sadly not as common as it once was following a decline in wild populations. This is a plant closely associated with folklore and tradition, as the flowers were picked and added to scented garlands during May Day celebrations.

The pretty yellow, sweetly scented, tubular flower is encased in a long, pale green calyx with a bell-shaped arrangement of petals, each with an orange spot at its base. The flowers hang down in a nodding, one-sided cluster at the top of a tall slender stem borne from a basal rosette of dark green, wrinkly leaves.

As pretty as cowslips are, their common name derives from 'cow slop', because of the plant's association with cow pats in the meadows and fields where it is commonly found.

Cowslips are wonderful plants for naturalising in lawns and meadows, where they will slowly increase and are beneficial to many bee species.

ASPECT: Full sun to partial shade.
FLOWERING: April–May.
SCENT: Light.
HARDINESS: -10 to -15 °C (14 to 5 °F).

15–25 cm (6–10 in)
15–25 cm (6–10 in)

PRIMULA VULGARIS
Primrose
PRIMULACEAE

A low-growing rosette of dark green, wrinkly leaves with hairy undersides provides an ideal backdrop to the primrose's clusters of pale-yellow flowers. Each of their petals is notched at its tip, with darker yellow or orange markings at its base.

In the wild, primroses are most commonly seen growing on woodland edges and the grassy edges of hedgerows along country lanes and it is in this kind of setting that they are best grown in gardens – somewhere that affords them damp, dappled shade. Here they will self-seed and naturalise.

Primroses are one of the first of the woodland wildflowers to bloom in the year and in some mild winters can be found in flower as early as late December. They are a great source of nectar and pollen for early foraging insects.

ASPECT: Partial shade.
FLOWERING: March–May.
SCENT: Light.
HARDINESS: -10 to -15 °C (14 to 5 °F).

5–10 cm (2–4 in)
20–30 cm (8–12 in)

Primula veris

Primula vulgaris

VIOLA ODORATA
Sweet violet
VIOLACEAE

This charming little plant will slowly spread via its rhizomes, naturalising in small areas, and is best grown where it can enjoy dappled shade, hopefully spreading to make a low-growing, loose carpet of ground cover.

The foliage is semi-evergreen, making small clusters of glossy green, heart-shaped leaves, with the flowers held on short, arching stems above the leaves. The violet-blue, occasionally white, sweetly fragrant little flowers nod at the tips of each stem.

The flowers of sweet violets are edible and can be used in salads and as cake decorations and for centuries they have been used in perfumery.

ASPECT: Partial shade.
FLOWERING: February–April.
SCENT: Medium.
HARDINESS: -10 to -15 °C (14 to 5 °F).

10–20 cm (4–8 in)
25–30 cm (10–12 in)

ZALUZIANSKYA OVATA
Night-scented phlox
SCROPHULARIACEAE

This is definitely a plant best grown on or near a patio, whether in a bed or container, as it releases the sweet scent from its flowers through the evening and into the night.

It also has aromatic, semi-evergreen foliage that grows to produce a neat, bushy dome with the flowers held well above it on long slender stems. The closed flower buds are a deep pink, opening in the evening to reveal pure white flowers with a small yellow centre, closing back up to tight buds the following morning.

Zaluzianskya ovata

Although not reliably hardy, it is definitely worth growing if you have a free-draining soil that doesn't sit wet in the winter. Alternatively, grow it in a container that can be kept frost-free in the winter.

Once it has finished flowering it should be cut back hard.

ASPECT: Full sun.
FLOWERING: June–September.
SCENT: Strong.
HARDINESS: 1 to -5 °C (34 to 23 °F).

20–30 cm (8–12 in)
30–60 cm (12–24 in)

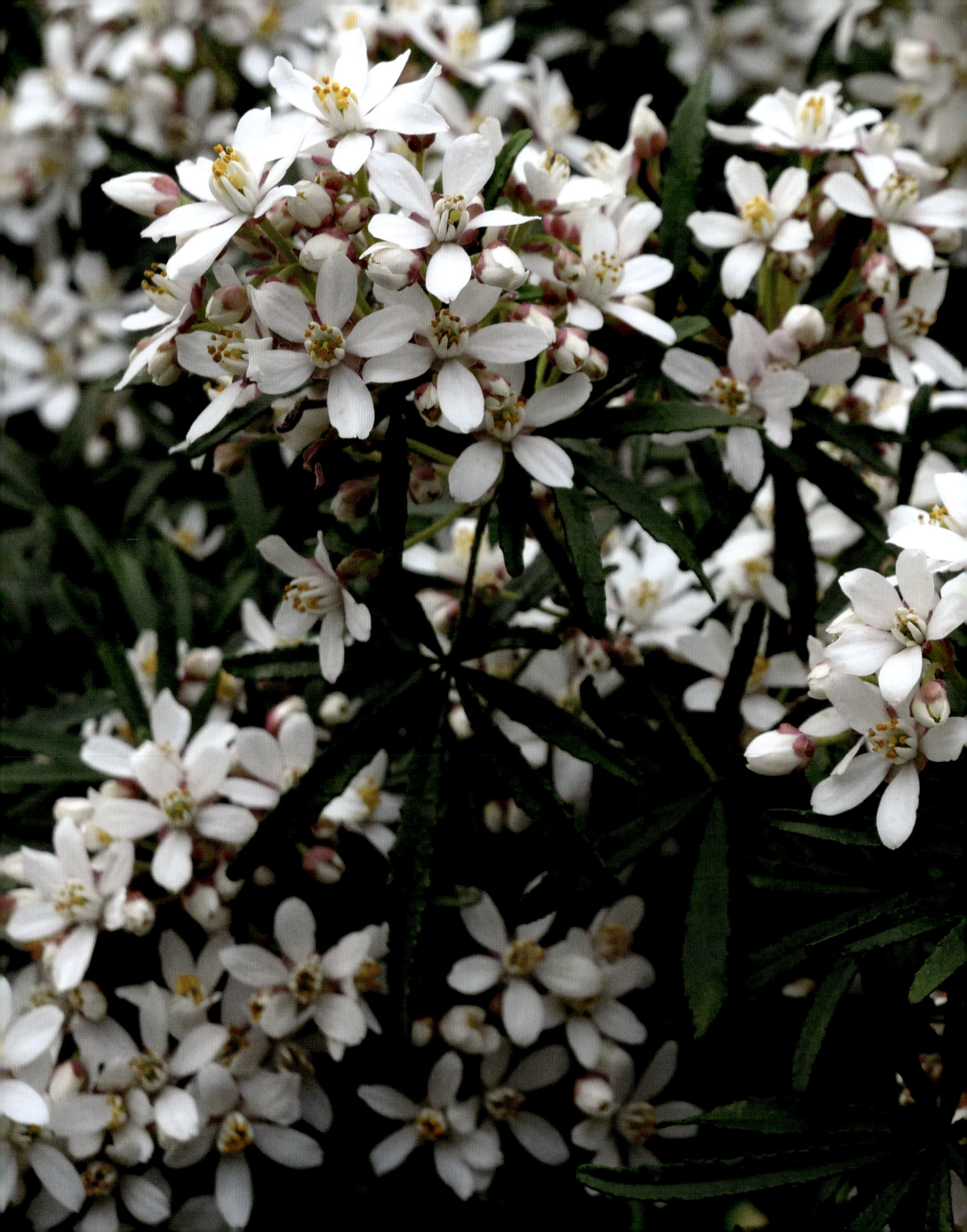

Shrubs

ABELIA × GRANDIFLORA
Glossy abelia
CAPRIFOLIACEAE

This is a medium-sized, evergreen or semi-evergreen shrub that is a cross between *Abelia chinensis* and *A. uniflora*. It produces arching stems with attractive glossy, dark green leaves that are kept all year except in the coldest years. The white, pink-tinged, trumpet-like flowers are produced over a long period through the summer and into early autumn. They have a light fragrance and are profuse, standing out well against the dark foliage.

Abelia grows well as a free-standing shrub but can also be trained against a wall, tying in the laterals as they develop.

Pruning should be carried out after flowering. If necessary, the oldest stems can be cut back hard to their base in early spring to produce vigorous new shoots.

ASPECT: Full sun to partial shade.
FLOWERING: June–October.
SCENT: Light.
HARDINESS: -10 to -15 °C (14 to 5 °F).

1.5–2.5 m (5–8 ft)
1.5–2.5 m (5–8 ft)

ABELIOPHYLLUM DISTICHUM
White forsythia
OLEACEAE

This is a deciduous shrub that, although it is in the same family and despite its common name, is in a different genus from true forsythia.

It's a pretty shrub that can be a little straggly if left to grow freely. If trained and pruned correctly, though, it makes a wonderful addition to a scented garden, with its starry, four-petalled, fragrant white flowers produced in abundance early in the year all along its bare, purplish stems, filling the air with beautiful fragrance.

White forsythia is not commonly seen in gardens, but because of its attractiveness and early flowering it is a plant that is definitely worth its space in any garden.

It is best grown against a sunny wall where its early flowers will get some protection from the coldest weather. This also shows off its flowers to best effect.

Pruning should be done after flowering so that new growth can be produced for the following year's flowering.

Abelia × grandiflora

Abeliophyllum distichum

ASPECT: Full sun to partial shade.
FLOWERING: February–March.
SCENT: Medium.
HARDINESS: -10 to -15 °C (14 to 5 °F).

1.5–2 m (5–7 ft)
1.5–2 m (5–7 ft)

ARGYROCYTISUS BATTANDIERI
Moroccan broom

FABACEAE

This is a medium-sized deciduous shrub with the most amazing silvery foliage. The leaves are trifoliate with a soft and silky sheen when young due to a covering of fine hairs, which also cover the stems.

Its bright yellow, pea-like flowers are produced in erect panicles on the tips of most of the stems. The flowers not only look like small pineapples but also smell of pineapple. Another common name for this plant is the pineapple broom.

It makes a handsome, rounded shrub that does best in full sun, and also makes a good wall shrub.

Any pruning should be carried out after flowering.

Argyrocytisus battandieri

ASPECT: Full sun.
FLOWERING: June–July.
SCENT: Medium.
HARDINESS: -10 to -15 °C (14 to 5 °F).

2–4 m (7–13 ft)
2–4 m (7–13 ft)

AZARA MICROPHYLLA
Box leaf azara

SALICACEAE

This is usually described as a large, evergreen, upright shrub, but in time – given good growing conditions – it may grow into a small tree. As its common name suggests, it has leaves that are small, very dark glossy green, and rounded, similar to those of the common box, *Buxus sempervirens*.

Individually, the flowers are tiny and almost insignificant, but *en masse* they stand out well against the dark foliage, and the scent they produce is amazing. It is a fragrance you will detect long before you realise where it is coming from.

The clusters of highly scented, dainty, bright yellow blooms are produced all along the stems between the leaf axils, making this a showy shrub.

As well as a free-standing specimen it will also make a good, trained wall shrub.

There is also a variegated form, **'Variegata'**, that has glossy green leaves with cream-coloured margins.

Prune lightly straight after flowering, if needed, to allow for good new growth as this will be what produces the flowers the following season.

Azara microphylla

SHRUBS 83

Azara 'Variegata'

ASPECT: Full sun to partial shade.
FLOWERING: January–March.
SCENT: Strong.
HARDINESS: -5 to -10 °C (23 to 14 °F).

4–6 m (13–20 ft)
3–4 m (10–13 ft)

AZARA SERRATA
Saw-toothed azara
SALICACEAE

This is an upright, evergreen, medium-sized shrub that will benefit from a sheltered position in full sun, where it will flower at its best.

Azara serrata has much larger, oval, glossy green leaves than the box leaf azara. They are also much sparser, which allows the numerous clusters of golden-yellow flowers, which have a marzipan scent, to been seen much more easily. After a hot summer, these are followed by white berries.

This is a great plant for bees and butterflies.

Azara serrata

Prune lightly straight after flowering, if needed, to allow for good new growth, as this will be what produces the flowers the following season.
ASPECT: Full sun to partial shade.
FLOWERING: May–June.
SCENT: Medium.
HARDINESS: -5 to -10 °C (23 to 14 °F).

2.5–4 m (8–13 ft)
1–3 m (5–10 ft)

BERBERIS MICROPHYLLA
Box-leaved barberry
BERBERIDACEAE

This is a plant that I didn't realise was fragrant until one day, as I was walking close to it, I picked up a scent and wasn't sure which plant it was coming from. I soon traced it to a pretty flowering berberis festooned with small, bright orange flowers, each hanging from a short pedicel all along its spiny stems.

The small, rounded, box-like, evergreen leaves are where the common name

Berberis microphylla

84   GARDENING WITH SCENTED PLANTS

comes from. The flowers are produced singly from leafy nodes, each like a little bell below an umbrella of paler petals.

Very little pruning will be required with this shrub, but any pruning that is needed should be carried out in late spring or early summer immediately after flowering has finished. Thorn-proof gloves should be worn when pruning berberis as they are armed with needle-like spines.

ASPECT: Full sun to partial shade.
FLOWERING: March–April.
SCENT: Medium.
HARDINESS: -5 to -10 °C (23 to 14 °F).

1.5–2.5 m (5–8 ft)
1.5–2.5 m (5–8 ft)

BUDDLEJA ALTERNIFOLIA
Fountain butterfly bush
SCROPHULARIACEAE

This is such a pretty *Buddleja* with long, slender, graceful, arching branches with narrow glaucous leaves that are silvery on their undersides. The pale purple or lilac flowers completely cover the arching stems in small, rounded, alternate clusters that spiral around the stems. They cascade like a fountain, which gives the plant the common name of the fountain butterfly bush, or fountain buddleja.

It is a very versatile shrub that can be trained into a small tree, or over an arch, as well as grown as a free-standing specimen shrub.

Because the flowers are produced on the previous year's shoots, it should be pruned straight after flowering, giving plenty of time for new growth to be made for next season's flowers.

ASPECT: Full sun.
FLOWERING: May–July.
SCENT: Medium.
HARDINESS: -10 to -15 °C (14 to 5 °F).

3–4 m (10–13 ft)
3–4 m (10–13 ft)

BUDDLEJA DAVIDII 'BLACK KNIGHT'
Butterfly bush
SCROPHULARIACEAE

There are many different cultivars of the butterfly bush, *Buddleja davidii*, but this cultivar is one of the most beautiful and highly scented.

Temperate species of *Buddleja* are all deciduous and their flowers come in many colours. 'Black Knight' is particularly attractive with its dense spikes of honey-scented, dark purple flowers, each with an orange centre. Like all *Buddleja* it is very attractive to butterflies.

Pruning should be carried out in early spring, removing the previous season's growth, back to three or four buds. Pruning a third of the bush at a time, at three- or four-week intervals, will extend the flowering season well into October. Deadheading will reduce the number of unwanted seedlings.

ASPECT: Full sun to partial shade.
FLOWERING: July–September.
SCENT: Medium.
HARDINESS: -10 to -15 °C (14 to 5 °F).

2–3 m (7–10 ft)
2–3 m (7–10 ft)

Buddleja alternifolia

Buddleja davidii 'Black Knight'

BUDDLEJA GLOBOSA
Orange ball tree
SCROPHULARIACEAE

The common name for this semi-deciduous large shrub is very apt, as it produces perfectly round, ball-shaped inflorescences in loose terminal clusters. Each distinctive inflorescence is made up of several small, sweet-scented flowers.

It is a great feature plant with its bright orange flowers and a great shrub for attracting bees and butterflies into the garden.

Being semi-evergreen, it will lose its leaves in very cold winters.

It is a shrub that needs very little maintenance apart from removing any dead branches. To reduce its size, remove the flowering shoots back to a strong bud. This also stops the plant getting too leggy, and should be done after flowering in late summer.

ASPECT: Full sun to partial shade.
FLOWERING: May–July.
SCENT: Medium.
HARDINESS: -10 to -15 °C (14 to 5 °F).

3–4 m (10–13 ft)
3–4 m (10–13 ft)

Buddleja globosa

BUDDLEJA SALVIIFOLIA
South African sage wood
SCROPHULARIACEAE

This is a semi-evergreen shrub with an arching habit and long, narrow panicles of sweetly fragrant, pale lilac flowers, each with a yellow-orange throat. It blooms in mid-summer.

As its common name suggests, it has foliage that is sage-like, covered in short, fine hairs, giving an overall greyish appearance. It is best planted in a sheltered, sunny spot out of cold winter winds.

Like all buddlejas this is a great plant to attract bees and butterflies into your garden.

Pruning should be carried out immediately after flowering.

ASPECT: Full sun to partial shade.
FLOWERING: October–November.
SCENT: Medium.
HARDINESS: 0 to -5 °C (32 to 23 °F).

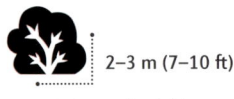

2–3 m (7–10 ft)
1.5–2.5 m (5–8 ft)

BUDDLEJA × WEYERIANA 'SUNGOLD'
Butterfly bush 'Sungold'
SCROPHULARIACEAE

The deciduous hybrid *Buddleja* 'Sungold' has been produced from a sport (a chance genetic mutation) of 'Golden Glow', which in turn is an earlier cross of two other fragrant buddlejas, *Buddleja davidii* and *Buddleja globosa*. It has small, golden-yellow, trumpet-like tubular flowers with a darker orange throat, which are produced in loose clusters borne along the ends of its long arching branches. Its leaves, too, are attractive – dark matt green above and silvery-grey underneath with a soft covering of tiny hairs, which also cover the new growth on the flowering stems.

Calycanthus floridus

Chimonanthus praecox

Pruning is similar to that of *Buddleja davidii* and should be carried out in early spring. It can be quite hard, if necessary, almost back to the base.
ASPECT: Full sun to partial shade.
FLOWERING: July–September.
SCENT: Medium.
HARDINESS: -10 to -15 °C (14 to 5 °F).

2–3 m (7–10 ft)
2–3 m (7–10 ft)

CALYCANTHUS FLORIDUS
Carolina allspice
CALYCANTHACEAE
This medium to large deciduous shrub, which has a dense, busy habit, has flowers, leaves and bark that are all fragrant, each with their own distinct scent. The deep red, almost brownish, magnolia-like flowers are produced singly, standing out well against the darker green leaves. Their fragrance seems to change with the weather – the stronger the sun and warmth, the stronger their scent.

Different scents are picked up by different people, including strawberry, pineapple and cinnamon. For me, the flowers have a light, spicy scent, the leaves camphor, and the bark a lemony cinnamon.

Prune immediately after flowering, if needed, to reduce its size or change its shape.
ASPECT: Full sun to partial shade.
FLOWERING: June–July.
SCENT: Light.
HARDINESS: -10 to -15 °C (14 to 5 °F).

2–3 m (7–10 ft)
2–3 m (7–10 ft)

CHIMONANTHUS PRAECOX
Winter sweet
CALYCANTHACEAE
This pretty, deciduous shrub displays its highly fragrant flowers during the winter months along leafless stems.

The waxy, bowl-shaped flowers can be quite variable in colour between different plants, but are generally creamy-white to yellow, hanging down in small clusters. Their scent fills the air around the plant, even when it is frost-covered.

There are two main cultivars, *Chimonanthus praecox* 'Grandiflorus', which has larger flowers that are yellow, often with a reddish centre, and *C. praecox* 'Luteus', which opens slightly later in the season and has rich yellow flowers.

Winter sweet is an ideal plant for training as a wall shrub and should only be pruned regularly once it has produced a mature branch system, immediately after flowering.
ASPECT: Full sun.
FLOWERING: December–February.
SCENT: Strong.
HARDINESS: -10 to -15 °C (14 to 5 °F).

1.5–3 m (3–10 ft)
1–1.5 m (3–5 ft)

Chimonanthus praecox 'Luteus'

SHRUBS 87

CHIONANTHUS VIRGINICUS
Fringe tree
OLEACEAE

This is a large, deciduous shrub that can eventually grow into a small tree, although it is relatively slow-growing. It may be one for the enthusiast as it can be difficult to obtain, but well worth the effort.

The unusual, creamy-white flowers are produced in panicles, each made up of several individual flowers that look spectacular when in full bloom. The flowers have four long, slightly twisted, drooping petals, and a delicate fragrance.

They are dioecious, having male and female flowers on different plants. Although the male flowers are larger, the female flowers can be followed by dark blue fruits in late summer.

This shrub also has the benefit of golden-yellow autumn colour.

Only minimal pruning is necessary and should be carried out in the dormant season, from late winter until early spring, when you can remove the lower limbs if you want a more tree-like plant.

ASPECT: Full sun.
FLOWERING: May–June.
SCENT: Light.
HARDINESS: -10 to -15 °C (14 to 5 °F).

2–3 m (7–10 ft)
2–3 m (7–10 ft)

Chionanthus virginicus

CHOISYA TERNATA
Mexican orange blossom
RUTACEAE

An ornamental evergreen shrub with fragrant flowers and foliage, Mexican orange blossom has been a favourite in many gardens for decades.

The main flush of starry white, scented flowers is produced in late spring against a backdrop of glossy green foliage, but it will flower on and off all summer and will usually produce a second flush at the end of the summer, giving year-round interest. The flowers almost cover the whole of the plant and have a fragrance similar to orange blossom, as the common name suggests.

The aromatic, dark green leaves have three leaflets (hence the species' Latin name *ternata* meaning 'in threes'), and when crushed smell like basil.

The cultivar **'Sundance'** has bright golden-yellow foliage and also produces fragrant white flowers.

Another cultivar that has a strong fragrance is **'Aztec Pearl'** which is a hybrid cross with striking evergreen foliage, producing a mass of pink buds that transform into fragrant, pure white flowers. It often has a second flush of flowers in the summer.

These are all very versatile shrubs that will also make a stunning flowering hedge, as they cope well with continual pruning. Prune after the first main flush of flowering is over in late spring.

Choisya ternata

Choisya × dewitteana 'Aztec Pearl'

Choisya 'Sundance'

ASPECT: Full sun to partial shade.
FLOWERING: May–June, with a second flush in late summer.
SCENT: Medium.
HARDINESS: -10 to -15 °C (14 to 5 °F).

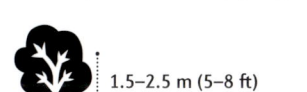

1.5–2.5 m (5–8 ft)
1.5–2.5 m (5–8 ft)

CISTUS LADANIFER
Gum rockrose

CISTACEAE

The gum rockrose is a striking, upright, evergreen shrub from the Mediterranean that is surprisingly hardy and very drought-tolerant.

This is a very showy shrub that during the summer months produces large white flowers, around 10 cm (4 in) across, which can be plain or have purple blotches at the base of each petal. Each flower only lasts a day, usually falling in mid-afternoon. They are replaced the following day with a whole new flush of flowers, which continues all summer.

During the hottest part of the year the foliage of this cistus exudes a sticky resin that turns the leaves from a dark, dull green to a glossy green as it covers their surface. This resin, known as labdanum, is highly aromatic and has been used in perfumes and herbal remedies for centuries. Its scent always reminds me of warm summer days.

Cistus creticus is a much shorter and more compact plant with pink flowers and foliage that is scented, particularly in hot weather, but not as fragrant as *C. ladanifer*.

Pruning should be done after flowering, if needed, but never into the old, ripened wood, as the plant does not respond well to hard pruning.

ASPECT: Full sun.
FLOWERING: June–August.
SCENT: Medium.
HARDINESS: -10 to -15 °C (14 to 5 °F).

1.5–3 m (5–10 ft)
1–1.5 m (3–5 ft)

CLERODENDRUM BUNGEI
Rose glory bower
LAMIACEAE

This is a great medium-sized shrub for late-season flowering in a border. The one downside is that it tends to sucker freely, so these need to be removed as they appear. Alternatively it can be grown in a container.

It is a fairly unusual deciduous shrub that produces dark green, heart-shaped, deeply veined leaves with a pungent scent when crushed. Its pretty, rose-pink flowers, on the other hand, are sweetly scented and borne in dense, dome-topped clusters from deep pink buds. The star-shaped flowers have long, showy stamens that protrude from their centre.

Being late flowering, it is a beneficial plant for late-foraging pollinators, which feed on its nectar.

In colder areas it can be killed down to ground level, but will regrow in the spring, so foliage left over winter for protection should be cut back in spring after the risk of frosts has passed.

ASPECT: Full sun to partial shade.
FLOWERING: August–October.
SCENT: Medium.
HARDINESS: -5 to -10 °C (23 to 14 °F).

1.5–2 m (5–7 ft)
1.5–2 m (5–7 ft)

Cistus ladanifer

Clerodendrum bungei

Clerodendrum trichotomum

Clethra alnifolia

CLERODENDRUM TRICHOTOMUM
Harlequin glorybower
LAMIACEAE

This is a large, deciduous shrub with an upright habit that in time will make a small tree. Its pretty white, star-shaped flowers are produced in the second half of the summer and have a fragrance strong enough to fill the surrounding air.

The white flowers emerge from terminal clusters of pink buds. Extending the seasonal interest, after the flowering is over bright blue berries are produced, surrounded by star-shaped, dark red, maroon calyces.

Care should be taken when weeding around this shrub as damage to the roots can result in suckering.

Pruning should be carried out regularly in early spring, shortening the previous year's growth back to two buds, which will help improve flowering.
ASPECT: Full sun to partial shade.
FLOWERING: July–September.
SCENT: Strong.
HARDINESS: -5 to -10 °C (23 to 14 °F).

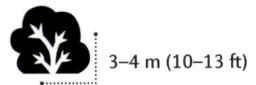

3–4 m (10–13 ft)
3–4 m (10–13 ft)

CLETHRA ALNIFOLIA
Sweet pepper bush
CLETHRACEAE

This is an unusual shrub and not one that is commonly grown, but it has good ornamental value for growing in a mixed border.

It is a medium-sized shrub with pretty white, fragrant racemes of upright flowers, which sit as terminal growths above the foliage in mid-summer. Each flower spike opens from the bottom upwards. It is very attractive to both bees and butterflies and has the added appeal of rich, golden-yellow autumnal colour.

There is a pink variety, *Clethra alnifolia* 'Ruby Spice'.

Very little pruning is necessary other than removing dead and damaged wood in spring. It does sucker so needs checking to keep under control.
ASPECT: Full sun to partial shade.
FLOWERING: July–August.
SCENT: Medium.
HARDINESS: -5 to -10 °C (23 to 14 °F).

1.5–2 m (5–7 ft)
1.5–2 m (5–7 ft)

CLETHRA BARBINERVIS
Japanese clethra
CLETHRACEAE

This is large deciduous shrub with dark green, oval leaves during the summer months that later in the year will provide good autumn yellows and reds. On mature speciments, attractive peeling bark is most visible after the leaves have fallen.

The flowers are produced in long, terminal, clustered sprays of small white, fragrant, open cup-shaped flowers, with showy protruding stamens from late summer, when most other woodland

Clethra barbinervis

SHRUBS 91

shrubs have finished flowering. The flowers are followed by dark brown, spike-shaped fruits.

Minimal pruning should be necessary apart from removing dead, damaged or crossing branches, and should be carried out in late winter or early spring while the shrub is dormant.

ASPECT: Full sun to partial shade.
FLOWERING: July–August.
SCENT: Medium.
HARDINESS: -5 to -10 °C (23 to 14 °F).

2–3 m (7–10 ft)
2–3 m (7–10 ft)

COLLETIA HYSTRIX
Bristly colletia
RHAMNACEAE

Definitely not one for the front of a border or along a path edge, but this large, spiny shrub has the most gloriously scented flowers. It is almost leafless and covered in grey-green, needle-sharp, rigid, round-tipped spines. While it is not the most attractive plant, when it flowers its fragrance can be intoxicating and the buzz of bees quite amazing. They are attracted to the small white, bell-shaped flowers borne in small clusters of twos and threes covering the spines.

A pink form, *Colletia hystrix* **'Rosea'**, is also available.

Minimal pruning is needed apart from cutting out dead, wayward or congested branches, and this should be carried out in late winter or early spring.

ASPECT: Full sun.
FLOWERING: July–October.
SCENT: Strong.
HARDINESS: -5 to -10 °C (23 to 14 °F).

2–4 m (7–13 ft)
2.5–4 m (8–10 ft)

CORONILLA VALENTINA SUBSP. *GLAUCA*
Glaucous scorpion-vetch
FABACEAE

This small, compact, evergreen shrub from the Mediterranean never ceases to amaze me with it hardiness, drought tolerance and ability to have some flowers on it even during the winter months.

Its glaucous green leaves contrast well with its bright golden-yellow, pea-like flowers, which have a rich lemon scent and are produced in small terminal clusters all over the plant, making a very showy shrub that will lighten up any border. The flowers are followed by slender, curving segmented pods that have a soft spine-like tip, similar to that of a scorpion's tail, from which it gets its common name.

There is a very popular cultivar, **'Citrina'**, which has paler lemon-yellow flowers, which still have the rich sweet scent.

Colletia hystrix

Coronilla glauca

Coronilla 'Citrina'

Very little pruning is necessary other than removing any dead tips in spring back to living wood, and some of the oldest wood if needed to reduce its size.
ASPECT: Full sun to partial shade.
FLOWERING: February–April (main flush).
SCENT: Medium.
HARDINESS: -5 to -10 °C (23 to 14 °F).

1–1.5 m (3–5 ft)
1–1.5 m (3–5 ft)

CORYLOPSIS PAUCIFLORA
Winter hazel
HAMAMELIDACEAE

This deciduous shrub is in the same family as *Hamamelis* and *Parrotia*. Although flowering at a similar time, their flowers are very different. *Corylopsis* is naturally a woodland plant so will do very well in a shadier part of the garden where its late winter flowers will lighten up the area.

The flowers are pale yellow, bell-shaped and have a scent similar to that of primrose, or cowslip. They hang in pretty clusters from the bare branches before the new leaves appear, which are a rich bronze colour.

Any necessary pruning should be carried out after flowering, but care should be taken not to destroy the plant's wide, spreading natural habit.

Corylopsis pauciflora

ASPECT: Partial shade.
FLOWERING: February–March.
SCENT: Light.
HARDINESS: -5 to -10 °C (23 to 14 °F).

1–1.5 m (3–5 ft)
1–1.5 m (3–5 ft)

CYTISUS 'PORLOCK'
Broom
FABACEAE

This evergreen or semi-evergreen shrub is also occasionally found under the name of *Genista* 'Porlock'. Both *Cytisus* and *Genista* are commonly called brooms.

It is vigorous grower, producing a bushy plant with small, soft dark green leaves. When in flower the bright yellow, pea-like flowers open in profuse racemes covering the whole plant with their colour and producing a wonderful fragrance.

Although hardy, it will do better given the protection of a sunny wall or fence.

No pruning is required, other than removing any long stems and branches that are heavy with seed pods and falling out of the main framework.
ASPECT: Full sun to partial shade.
FLOWERING: April–June.
SCENT: Medium.
HARDINESS: -5 to -10 °C (23 to 14 °F).

1.5–2.5 m (5–8 ft)
1.5–2.5 m (5–8 ft)

DAPHNE BHOLUA
Nepalese paper plant
THYMELAEACEAE

This semi-evergreen or deciduous shrub – which has some of the most fragrant flowers of any flowering shrub – is mostly found in its many cultivar forms. The blooms are produced in terminal clusters of up to 20 highly fragrant flowers, which are reddish in bud, opening white, but keeping some of their reddish bud colour on the reverse of the petals. The flowers stand out well against their mid-green, leathery leaves.

The cultivar **'Alba'** is an upright evergreen or semi-evergreen plant that produces pure white flowers, opening from pale pink buds. **'Gurkha'** is a deciduous variety collected in Nepal in the early 1960s and is formally named *Daphne bholua* var. *glacialis* **'Gurkha'**. It is one of the oldest of the named cultivars, with pink flowers.

Probably the best-known cultivar is **'Jacqueline Postill'**, which is usually evergreen, except in the coldest winters, and has highly fragrant pink flowers. It originated from a seedling of 'Gurkha' raised in Hillier Nurseries in England.

Daphne bholua and its cultivars do not require any pruning, except for removing any dead or diseased wood, so they should be planted where there is room for them to grow to maturity.

ASPECT: Full sun to partial shade.
FLOWERING: January–March.
SCENT: Strong.
HARDINESS: -10 to -15 °C (14 to 5 °F).

1.5–2.5 m (5–8 ft)
1–1.5 m (3–5 ft)

DAPHNE LAUREOLA
Spurge laurel
THYMELAEACEAE

This is an evergreen shrub that has dark green, glossy leaves in clusters at the top of each stem and it is below these that the fragrant, yellow-green, tubular flowers are borne in small clusters on short stalks.

This is a great plant for growing in a shady area as it is naturally a woodland plant native to many parts of Europe, including the UK.

Daphne laureola subsp. *philippi* is a dwarf form with a rounded shape, similar in most ways to the species except in its size (50 cm wide x 50 cm tall). Its flowers are also smaller.

Daphne laureola does not require any pruning, except for removing any dead or diseased wood, so it should be planted where there is room for it to grow to maturity.

ASPECT: Full sun to partial shade.
FLOWERING: January–March.
SCENT: Light.
HARDINESS: -10 to -15 °C (14 to 5 °F).

1–1.5 m (3–5 ft)
1.5–2.5 m (5–8 ft)

Daphne 'Jacqueline Postill'

Daphne laureola

Daphne odora 'Aureomarginata'

Daphne mezereum

DAPHNE ODORA 'AUREOMARGINATA'
Golden-edged daphne

THYMELAEACEAE

This evergreen variegated shrub has a compact form so is ideal for growing in a smaller garden or restricted spot, doing particularly well in shade.

It is a very showy plant with its dark green, glossy leaves, edged with a golden-yellow margin, giving it year-round appeal. The fragrant pink flowers are produced in small terminal clusters in winter and add an extra element to this shrub with their sweet fragrance.

Another cultivar, **'Rogbret'**, has the same pink flowers, but its leaf margins have a wider creamy-white edge to them.

Daphne odora and its cultivars do not require any pruning, except for removing any dead or diseased wood, so should be planted where there is room for them to grow to maturity.

ASPECT: Full sun to partial shade.
FLOWERING: January–March.
SCENT: Medium.
HARDINESS: -5 to -10 °C (23 to 14 °F).

1–1.5 m (3–5 ft)
75 cm–1 m (30 in–3 ft)

DAPHNE MEZEREUM
Mezereon

THYMELAEACEAE

An early and attractive plant, like most of the daphnes, mezereon will do well in shade, as it is naturally a woodland plant. It is deciduous and bears all of its lilac or purplish-coloured, fragrant flowers clustered along its bare stems, before the foliage appears. These are followed by bright scarlet berries.

There is also a white-flowered form, ***Daphne mezereum* f. *alba***, in which the blooms are followed by yellow berries.

Daphne mezereum and its cultivars do not require any pruning, except for removing any dead or diseased wood. They should be planted where there is room for them to grow to maturity.

ASPECT: Full sun to partial shade.
FLOWERING: February–March.
SCENT: Medium.
HARDINESS: -10 to -15 °C (14 to 5 °F).

1–1.5 m (3–5 ft)
1–1.5 m (3–5 ft)

DIPELTA FLORIBUNDA
Rosy dipelta
CAPRIFOLIACEAE

Given time, this deciduous shrub can become quite large and will need space to grow, so is more suited to a larger garden. With maturity, the larger stems will produce a flaking and peeling bark, giving winter interest once the leaves have fallen.

The clusters of flowers are white or soft pink and bell-shaped, separated into five lobes which have an orange lower section and throat. These showy flowers are sweetly fragrant.

The green bracts at the base of each flower are attractive in their own right, turning from green to pink and bronze after flowering.

Any pruning that is necessary should be carried out after flowering.

ASPECT: Full sun to partial shade.
FLOWERING: April–June.
SCENT: Medium.
HARDINESS: -10 to -15 °C (14 to 5 °F).

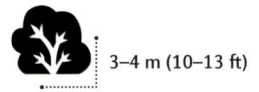

3–4 m (10–13 ft)
2–3 m (7–10 ft)

Edgeworthia 'Red Dragon'

EDGEWORTHIA CHRYSANTHA
Paperbush
THYMELAEACEAE

This is an unusual deciduous shrub, with a bushy but open, rounded habit, with papery brown bark and lush, lanceolate leaves that are produced on fresh green terminal stems. But it is on the previous season's woody growth that the rounded heads of flowers are borne before the new leaf growth.

It is for its flowers that this plant excels – rounded clusters of bright yellow, tubular flowers that open from white, silky-haired buds. The flowers appear on the tips of the bare stems in late winter, filling the air with their sweet scent.

The cultivar **'Grandiflora'** produces a larger plant with larger flowers, and **'Red Dragon'** has striking orange-red flowers that are particularly showy, flowering slightly later and lasting longer into early spring. Both plants are equally fragrant. No pruning should be required.

Edgeworthia chrysantha

ASPECT: Full sun to partial shade.
FLOWERING: February–April.
SCENT: Strong.
HARDINESS: -5 to -10 °C (23 to 14 °F).

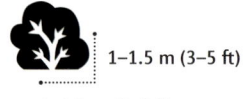

1–1.5 m (3–5 ft)
1–1.5 m (3–5 ft)

ELAEAGNUS × SUBMACROPHYLLA
Oleaster
ELAEAGNACEAE

This is a large, evergreen, densely branched shrub with bluish-green, glaucous leaves. It used to be known as *Elaeagnus × ebbingei* and will probably continue to be for some time. A hybrid, its parents were *E. macrophylla* and *E. pungens*.

It produces clusters of small, silvery-white or cream flowers in the autumn that last well into winter, giving off a strong fragrance, particularly when the air is still. These are followed by red fruits in late spring.

The dense growth and its ability to be hard-pruned make this fragrant shrub ideal for use as a hedge or screen. Pruning should be carried out in early summer.
ASPECT: Full sun to partial shade.
FLOWERING: October–November.
SCENT: Strong.
HARDINESS: -10 to -15 °C (14 to 5 °F).

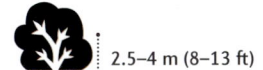

2.5–4 m (8–13 ft)
2.5–4 m (8–13 ft)

ELAEAGNUS UMBELLATA
Autumn olive
ELAEAGNACEAE

Elaeagnus umbellata is a deciduous shrub that has two main seasons of interest, one of which is springtime when its flowers fill the air with a deliciously sweet scent.

The creamy-white flowers are relatively small but are produced in profusion, in clusters among the oval-shaped leaves, which are dark green above and silvery beneath with a covering of fine hairs that also cover the young growth. The flowers are followed by a second season of interest in the autumn – bright red fruits that are speckled all over with tiny silvery dots.

The common name of autumn olive is slightly confusing because while the fruits are similar to small olives in shape, and are edible when fully ripe and rich in vitamin C, they are nothing like the colour of olives!

I think this is a very underrated shrub that should be planted more.

Minimal pruning is needed for this shrub. Regular pruning isn't needed and should be carried out after flowering, though this will mean less fruiting.
ASPECT: Full sun to partial shade.
FLOWERING: April–May.
SCENT: Strong.
HARDINESS: -10 to -15 °C (14 to 5 °F).

2.5–4 m (8–13 ft)
2.5–4 m (8–13 ft)

ERICA ARBOREA
Tree heather
ERICACEAE

This upright, evergreen, bushy shrub is commonly known as the tree heather because it can grow quite tall, but it is always multi-stemmed and almost as wide as it is tall. Its leaves are dark green and needle-like. Flowers are produced *en masse* in large terminal clusters. Each of the tiny, pure white individual flowers is bell-shaped, with brown anthers. The sweetly scented flowers cover most of the shrub and fill the immediate area around it with honey-like fragrance.

The cultivar **'Albert's Gold'** has golden yellow foliage, and is more compact, growing to around 2 m tall. Its flowers are fragrant, but it is not as floriferous as the species and is mainly grown for foliage colour.

Although this shrub can be found growing wild in parts of the Mediterranean, it is fully hardy, and although it prefers acid soils, it will tolerate soils that are slightly alkaline.

Elaeagnus × submacrophylla

Erica arborea

Like most evergreen shrubs, *Erica arborea* needs minimal pruning. Any that is needed should be carried out after flowering.
ASPECT: Full sun.
FLOWERING: February–April.
SCENT: Strong.
HARDINESS: -10 to -15 °C (14 to 5 °F).

2.5–4 m (8–13 ft)
2.5–4 m (8–13 ft)

ESCALLONIA ILLINITA
Escallonia
ESCALLONIACEAE

Grown for its attractive shiny evergreen foliage and white tubular flowers, this medium-sized shrub also gives off the most amazing, strong fragrance.

I can remember passing it in the arboretum at Kew and wondering which plant was producing such a strong scent, as I could see no visible flower close by. Later I was to learn that it was the sticky, aromatic leaves of *Escallonia*. The scent always seems stronger in the autumn, but it is fragrant all year round.

As well as a stand-alone garden plant, this shrub also makes an ideal hedging plant and is very tolerant of coastal salt spray.

Prune after flowering.
ASPECT: Full sun.
FLOWERING: June–July.
SCENT: Strong.
HARDINESS: -10 to -15 °C (14 to 5 °F).

1.5–2.5 m (5–8 ft)
1.5–2.5 m (5–8 ft)

FICUS CARICA
Edible fig
MORACEAE

This is a large deciduous shrub that, if left unpruned, will develop into a wide and spreading small tree. It has been with us since the Romans introduced it from the Middle East, where it is native.

The large, leathery, rounded, lobed leaves are immediately identifiable, and it is these and the fruits that produce the aroma that fills the air in close proximity to the plant during hot summer's days. Its flowers are tiny and insignificant.

The edible fig is ideal for training on a wall or fence where its growth can be controlled. Ideally its roots should also be controlled by keeping them containerised. This helps with fruit production, rather than just leaf production.

It is fully drought tolerant once established.

Any pruning should be carried out in spring once all risk of frost has passed. Care should be taken as the white, resinous sap can be an irritant to some.
ASPECT: Full sun to partial shade.
FLOWERING: Insignificant.
SCENT: Medium.
HARDINESS: -10 to -15 °C (14 to 5 °F).

2.5–5 m (8–16 ft)
3–5 m (10–16 ft)

Escallonia illinita

Ficus carica

Hamamelis × intermedia 'Angelly'

Heptacodium miconioides

HAMAMELIS × INTERMEDIA
Chinese witch hazel
HAMAMELIDACEAE

The different species of hamamelis, *Hamamelis mollis* and *Hamamelis vernalis*, both produce spicy-scented flowers. But it is the hybrid *Hamamelis × intermedia* that has the most available cultivars in a range of colours from the palest of yellows through to oranges and vibrant reds. Many of these also have a sweet or spicy scent.

'**Angelly**' has a light scent with beautiful pale, primrose-yellow flowers that almost cover the entire bare stems. '**Jelena**' produces coppery-red flowers that are sweetly scented and provide good autumnal colour.

They are all deciduous and produce their spidery flowers in late winter and on until early spring.

All these hybrid cultivars are grafted, so any suckers that are produced below the graft union should be removed, as these are very vigorous and if left will lead to reversion and weakening of the cultivar.
ASPECT: Full sun to partial shade.
FLOWERING: December–March.
SCENT: Medium
HARDINESS: -10 to -15 °C (14 to 5 °F).

2–4 m (6–13 ft)
2–4 m (6–13 ft)

HEPTACODIUM MICONIOIDES
Seven sons tree
CAPRIFOLIACEAE

This unusual large shrub is in a 'monotypic' genus, meaning that it only has this one species. Although it will make a small tree, it is classed as a shrub because it is naturally multi-stemmed.

It has an upright, bushy habit with attractive bark on the more mature stems that is yellowish brown and peels in long strips, revealing the lighter bark underneath. The tips of the branches are covered with small white, fragrant, star-like flowers from late summer into autumn that are very popular with butterflies and other insects. As the flowers fall, they leave behind bright red calyces, which are attractive in their own right.

Any pruning should be carried out in early spring. Lifting some of the lower branches will help expose the attractive peeling mature stems.
ASPECT: Full sun–partial shade.
FLOWERING: August–September.
SCENT: Medium.
HARDINESS: -10 to -15 °C (14 to 5 °F).

4–6 m (13–20 ft)
2–4 m (6.5–13 ft)

HOHERIA GLABRATA
Mountain ribbonwood
MALVACEAE

This is a large, deciduous shrub or small tree with a pendulous habit, becoming more so when in flower. In New Zealand, where it is native to the South Island, it is spring flowering, but in the UK it produces flowers in profusion from mid- to late summer, when few other shrubs are flowering.

Its pendulous habit allows the large, five-petalled, fragrant white flowers to hang attractively, each on individual stems but grouped in small clusters, contrasting well with the glabrous foliage.

Pruning is only necessary to parts that may have been damaged during winter.

ASPECT: Full sun to partial shade.
FLOWERING: July–August.
SCENT: Medium.
HARDINESS: -10 to -15 °C (14 to 5 °F).

2.5–4 m (8–13 ft)
2.5–4 m (8–13 ft)

ITEA ILICIFOLIA
Holly-leaf sweetspire
ITEACEAE

Grown against a wall or fence, this medium-sized evergreen shrub is particularly showy, although as a standalone specimen it will do equally well. It is relatively slow-growing but definitely worth the wait for the spectacular plant it becomes once mature, when it will not fail to impress.

It has glossy, dark green, holly-like leaves that can be almost hidden by the long flowering spikes in summer, which hang down like catkins and can be up to 30 cm (12 in) long, with many tiny, honey-scented, greenish-white flowers.

Grown as a wall shrub it will need wire supports, regular tying in and some pruning of the new shoots. As a specimen shrub very little pruning is necessary, apart from removing dead or damaged wood. It is best pruned after flowering.

ASPECT: Full sun to partial shade.
FLOWERING: July–August.
SCENT: Medium.
HARDINESS: -10 to -15 °C (14 to 5 °F).

2.5–4 m (8–13 ft)
2.5–4 m (8–13 ft)

Hoheria glabrata

Itea ilicifolia

ITEA VIRGINICA
Virginian sweet spire
ITEACEAE

This is a small, bushy, deciduous shrub with erect branches that become pendulous when in flower.

The fragrant, creamy-white flowers are produced in mid-summer as long terminal spikes that are slightly curved. Each spike is made up of dozens of small individual flowers that open from the base of the spike, each having a long flowering period.

Naturally found growing in woodland, this is a plant that will do best in a semi-shady spot.

The cultivar **'Henry's Garnet'**, as well as having fragrant summer flowers, is known for its attractive red/purple autumn colour.

Prune after flowering to maintain the bushy habit and to encourage new healthy growth.

ASPECT: Partial shade.
FLOWERING: May–July.
SCENT: Light.
HARDINESS: -10 to -15 °C (14 to 5 °F).

1.5–2.5 m (5–8 ft)
1–2 m (3–7 ft)

LAVANDULA
Lavender
LAMIACEAE

When it comes to summer-flowering scented plants, surely lavender is among the top ones, along with roses and lilacs. It is equally fragrant whether growing or cut and dried.

A small, evergreen shrub that has been grown for centuries for its aromatic, culinary and medicinal qualities, it is known to have been used in ancient Egypt as part of the process of mummification over 2,000 years ago.

The aromatic, grey-green leaves are covered in fine hairs, making them soft to the touch. The flowers are held on long, unbranched spikes above the foliage, in shades of violet-blue to purple. They open in succession over a period of weeks, but are already attractive weeks before this while in bud.

They are also low-maintenance and drought-tolerant once established, with flowers that are highly attractive to bees and butterflies for their rich supply of nectar. They also have culinary uses in flavouring food and drinks.

Regular pruning is a must, as once the plants get too woody, they not only look untidy but are also less likely to respond to hard pruning. Prune annually, cutting just below the bottom of the flower stalks, and of course the prunings will make excellent scented dried flowers.

There are dozens of cultivars for all of the different species, with new ones being raised all the time. I have only featured a few of each to show the range of colours.

LAVANDULA ANGUSTIFOLIA – Known as common or English lavender, this is probably the most popular species of lavender as it has the largest range of cultivars and colours. All are highly scented. They also work well grown in mixed borders, as edging plants, in containers and as low hedging.

The cultivar 'Hidcote' has deep violet-coloured flowers and remains a popular cultivar. It was named after Lawrence Johnston's Arts and Crafts garden in Gloucestershire. Another very popular cultivar is 'Munstead', also named after a garden, Munstead Wood, created by the famous plantswoman, Gertrude Jekyll.

Another good pink variety is 'Loddon Pink', which grows to approx. 50 cm x 50 cm (20 in x 20 in).

LAVANDULA × *INTERMEDIA* – Commonly called Lavandin, this is a hybrid cross between *L. angustifolia* and *L. latifolia*. It is highly fragrant with a range of attractive cultivars, and flowers that are generally larger than those of *L. angustifolia*. This is the lavender most commonly grown commercially for its oil, which is used in aromatherapy and perfumes, as well as for cut flowers.

The cultivar 'Grosso' has large flowerheads that are a rich purple colour. 'Edelweiss' has tall spikes of the palest pink or white flowers. Both cultivars will grow to 60 cm x 60 cm (24 in x 24 in).

LAVANDULA STOECHAS – Commonly called French lavender, this is quite different from other species of lavender, with shorter growth and chunkier flowerheads, each packed with small individual flowers in parallel lines, topped with four large and showy tufted bracts that can differ in colour from the main flowerhead. It isn't the hardiest lavender, but a sheltered, sunny pot with good drainage will get it through most winters. There is a large range of cultivars and colour variants, from whites through to pinks, reds, blues, and the deepest purple. It is definitely worth garden space.

'Kew Red' is a cultivar that has a ruby-red flower with pink bracts and aromatic grey-green foliage. 'Tiara' has deep blue flowers that are topped with cream-coloured bracts, and 'Snowman', as its name suggests, has pure white flowers with white bracts.

ASPECT: Full sun.
FLOWERING: June–September.
SCENT: Strong.
HARDINESS: -5 to -10 °C (23 to 14 °F).

40–60 cm (16–24 in)
40–60 cm (16–24 in)

Lavender

Ligustrum vulgare

LIGUSTRUM VULGARE
Common privet
OLEACEAE

Common privet is probably not one of the first shrubs that comes to mind when selecting plants for their fragrance.

In Britian it is an evergreen or semi-evergreen plant most commonly used for hedging or as a boundary plant, regularly pruned to keep it tidy and in check. It is because of this regular pruning that it rarely gets a chance to produce flowers. But the family Oleaceae has many different plants that are highly fragrant, including the summer flowers of privet, which are white, tubular and borne in terminal clusters. They are very attractive to both bees and butterflies.

Pruning can be carried out most times of the year, but is best in early spring to provide for bird nesting, plus summer flowers, and black autumn berries.

ASPECT: Full sun to partial shade.
FLOWERING: June–August.
SCENT: Medium.
HARDINESS: -10 to -15 °C (14 to 5 °F).

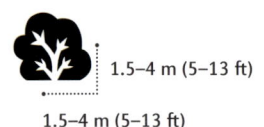

1.5–4 m (5–13 ft)
1.5–4 m (5–13 ft)

LONICERA FRAGRANTISSIMA
Winter honeysuckle
CAPRIFOLIACEAE

This pretty, medium-sized shrub can remain evergreen for many years, but in some winters it will lose a few, or all of its leaves. However, this has no effect on the development of its sweetly fragrant, creamy-white flowers, which are produced in pairs from late winter into early spring.

There is also a hybrid between *Lonicera fragrantissima* and *L. standishii*. Its cultivar **Lonicera × purpusii 'Winter Beauty'** is similar to *L. fragrantissima* but has darker purple flowering stems and is generally more floriferous, though this does differ from year to year.

Pruning should be carried out after flowering if needed, reducing around one third of the oldest arching flowering stems.

ASPECT: Full sun to partial shade.
FLOWERING: December–March.
SCENT: Strong.
HARDINESS: -10 to -15 °C (14 to 5 °F).

1.5–2.5 m (5–8 ft)
1.5–2.5 m (5–8 ft)

MYRTUS COMMUNIS
Common myrtle
MYRTACEAE

This is a favourite of mine, as every part of this pretty, evergreen shrub is fragrant. It has an upright form with small, oval, glossy, dark green leaves that are fragrant when crushed. Its dark foliage is a good backdrop to other plants that are paler in colour, particularly in winter when it's not in flower.

In early summer, small, rounded pink buds are borne on individual stems, opening to produce the most wonderfully showy, pure white, sweetly scented flowers that cover the whole of the plan. When fully open they are filled with a mass of white stamens, topped with creamy-white anthers. The flowers are followed by bluish-black berries, which in Corsica and Sardinia are steeped in alcohol to produce liquors.

Very little if any pruning is needed.

ASPECT: Full sun.
FLOWERING: July–August.
SCENT: Medium.
HARDINESS: -10 to -15 °C (14 to 5 °F).

2–3 m (7–10 ft)
1.5–2 m (5–7 ft)

Lonicera fragrantissima

Myrtus communis

OSMANTHUS DELAVAYI
Sweet olive
OLEACEAE

This is a wonderful evergreen shrub with tiny, dark-green leaves with a serrated margin. From mid to late spring it becomes a rounded shrub with arching branches that carry clusters of small, pure white, sweetly scented, jasmine-like, tubular flowers along their length.

Osmanthus delavayi is one of the parents of the equally fragrant hybrid *Osmanthus × burkwoodii* (see below), which is usually slightly earlier flowering and generally makes a smaller shrub when mature.

This is a relatively slow-growing shrub that will need little or no pruning (except if grown as a hedge). Any pruning should be carried out in late spring after flowering has finished.
ASPECT: Full sun to partial shade.
FLOWERING: March–April.
SCENT: Strong.
HARDINESS: -10 to -15 °C (14 to 5 °F).

1.5–2.5 m (5–8 ft)
1.5–2.5 m (5–8 ft)

OSMANTHUS × BURKWOODII
Burkwood osmanthus
OLEACEAE

This evergreen shrub is a cross between *Osmanthus decorus* and *Osmanthus delavayi*. It has a dense and compact habit with small, dark green, finely toothed and shiny leaves, which make it a good year-round plant to use as a background to show off other plants, as well as its own flowers. It is these that make this a standout shrub – an abundance of small, white, tubular, four-petalled, highly fragrant blooms produced in clusters that cover the whole plant. Their intense fragrance fills the air for some distance from the plant.

This shrub will also take regular pruning, making it ideal as a fragrant flowering hedge.

It is relatively slow-growing so will need little or no pruning (except if grown as a hedge). Any necessary pruning should be carried out in late spring after flowering has finished.
ASPECT: Full sun to partial shade.
FLOWERING: March–April.
SCENT: Strong.
HARDINESS: -10 to -15 °C (14 to 5 °F).

2.5–3 m (8–10 ft)
2.5–3 m (8–10 ft)

Osmanthus delavayi

Osmanthus × burkwoodii

PHILADELPHUS
Mock orange
HYDRANGEACEAE

This is a huge genus comprising around 80 different deciduous species, plus many more cultivars, including some with variegated and yellow foliage. All have the common name mock orange. They are closely related to *Deutzia*, from which they differ in having four-petalled flowers while *Deutzia* has five. Even though the flowering period is quite short, they flower at a time of year when many other shrub flowers are past their best, which makes the mock orange an ideal shrub to fill that gap. Showy and fragrant, it's an ideal garden plant whether grown as a specimen in a lawn or as part of a mixed bed or border planting, which will fill the air with the fragrance of orange blossom on warm summer evenings.

PHILADELPHUS CORONARIUS – As its name suggests, the common mock orange is the commonest cultivated species. It makes a tall, upright plant with arching branches when in flower. The flowers are cup-shaped and creamy-white. This free-flowering species is a great plant for a wildlife garden and very attractive to bees and butterflies. 2.5 x 3 m (8 x 10 ft).

The cultivar 'Aureus' has bright yellow leaves when young that become greenish yellow with age, contrasting well with its pure white flowers. 'Variegatus' is noted for its variegated green foliage, each leaf with a creamy-white margin. 1.5 x 2.5 m (4 x 8ft).

Philadelphus 'Fragrant Falls' is one of the most fragrant of all of the cultivars, producing clusters of white, bell-shaped flowers that contrast with its dark green leaves. The flowers are borne along long, arching and trailing branches. 1.5 x 2.5 m (4 x 8ft).

PHILADELPHUS MICROPHYLLUS – This small-leaved mock orange is a compact, upright shrub with a twiggy habit. It is notable for its small size compared with other species, making it suitable for a smaller garden or space. It produces its four-petalled, single pure white, highly fragrant flowers in abundance in midsummer. It has the added attraction of having chestnut-brown peeling bark. 1 x 1 m (3 x 3 ft).

PHILADELPHUS 'LEMOINEI' is a stunning small hybrid that was produced in the late 19th century as a result of a cross between *P. coronarius* and *P. microphyllus*. It has relatively large flowers for its size, borne in clusters of 3–5, which are bright white with striking yellow stamens. 1.5 x 1.5 m (5 x 5 ft).

PHILADELPHUS 'VIRGINAL' is probably the best of the double-flowered cultivars. It has an abundance of beautifully scented, large, pure white, double flowers that are produced against a background of dark green foliage, which goes on to have yellowish autumnal tones. 2.5 x 3 m (8 x 10 ft).

All philadelphuses should be pruned immediately after flowering every few years, thinning out old flowering wood as low to the ground as possible.

ASPECT: Full sun to partial shade.
FLOWERING: June–July.
SCENT: Strong.
HARDINESS: -10 to -15 °C (14 to 5 °F).

1.5–2.5 m (5–8 ft)
1.5–2.5 m (5–8 ft)

Philadelphus coronarius

Philadelphus 'Fragrant Falls'

PRUNUS LAUROCERASUS
Cherry laurel
ROSACEAE

Often just grown as an evergreen boundary or a large screening hedge because of its rich green, glossy foliage, it also produces masses of candle-like, fragrant flower spikes that are made up of around 50 small and delicate, pure white, showy flowers. Each has five rounded petals, a ring of long stamens and a central protruding stigma. The flowers are followed by small, round, reddish fruits that turn black when ripe and are inedible to humans.

Cherry laurel is a very vigorous shrub, growing 30–60 cm (1–2 ft) a year, and therefore needs regular pruning to keep it in check as it will very quickly become tall and woody, making it difficult for many gardeners to deal with without professional equipment or help. But with seasonal pruning it can make a super dense hedge that is also drought tolerant.

The cultivar **'Otto Luykens'** is much more manageable for a small garden, growing to around 1 m (3 ft) tall with narrow, dark green, glossy leaves. Cherry laurel should be pruned in late spring after flowering.

ASPECT: Full sun to partial shade.
FLOWERING: March–April.
SCENT: Medium.
HARDINESS: -10 to -15 °C (14 to 5 °F).

3–8 m (10–26 ft)
3–4 m (10–13 ft)

Prunus laurocerasus

Prunus 'Otto Luykens'

PRUNUS LUSITANICA
Portuguese laurel
ROSACEAE

The Portuguese laurel develops into a large evergreen shrub or small tree (if left unpruned), with glossy, dark green foliage that contrasts well with both the new growth of red shoots and the long, hanging racemes of creamy-white, strongly fragrant flowers. These are followed by small red fruits that turn black once mature and are a source of late autumn food for birds, but toxic to humans.

This is a very versatile plant that can be trimmed as topiary, regularly pruned as a hedge, used as a screening plant or grown as a single specimen. It tolerates most soil types and quite heavy shade.

Pruning should be carried out from late spring to summer and can be hard if needed.

ASPECT: Full sun to partial shade.
FLOWERING: May–June.
SCENT: Medium.
HARDINESS: -10 to -15 °C (14 to 5 °F).

3–5 m (10–16 ft)
3–4 m (10–13 ft)

Prunus lusitanica

Rhododendron 'Loderi King George'

Rhododendron luteum

RHODODENDRON 'LODERI KING GEORGE'
Rhododendron
ERICACEAE

This large evergreen rhododendron is considered to be one of the finest hybrids ever raised and is a truly magnificent plant that in time will grow to the size of a small tree, so it will need plenty of space to grow to maturity and is not suited to a small garden. Its parents are *Rhododendron fortunei* and *R. griffithianum*. Both produce some fragrance, but neither as strong as their resulting hybrid.

Its large pink buds open to huge, trumpet-shaped white flowers that are flushed with pink and have pale green markings in the throat. They are produced in trusses of up to 12 flowers each and are highly fragrant, filling the air with their sweet scent.

Very little pruning is necessary, other than removing any dead or diseased wood from time to time should it appear.

ASPECT: Full sun to partial shade.
FLOWERING: March–April.
SCENT: Strong.
HARDINESS: -10 to -15 °C (14 to 5 °F).

2.5–4 m (8–13 ft)
2.5–3 m (8–10 ft)

RHODODENDRON LUTEUM
Yellow azalea
ERICACEAE

This is a species that has been in cultivation for many years and is a plant that was once regarded as a deciduous azalea, and may still be found under the name *Azalea pontica*.

It's a bushy shrub that is relatively fast-growing with flowers that are produced in profusion just as the plant comes into leaf from its sticky winter buds. The bright yellow, funnel-shaped flowers are sweetly fragrant and borne in terminal clusters.

During autumn the leaves can give a stunning display, turning orange, red and yellow.

Other fragrant, deciduous rhododendrons (azaleas) include *Rhododendron occidentale* (western azalea) and *Rhododendron viscosum* (swamp azalea). Both also produce good autumn colour.

Rhododendron luteum is best grown in full sun to maximise flowering potential and it prefers neutral to acid soils. Pruning is minimal, removing dead and damaged wood in spring.

ASPECT: Full sun.
FLOWERING: May–June.
SCENT: Strong.
HARDINESS: -10 to -15 °C (14 to 5 °F).

1.5–3 m (5–10 ft)
1.5–3 m (5–10 ft)

RIBES ODORATUM
Buffalo currant
GROSSULARIACEAE

This small to medium deciduous shrub may also be found under the name *Ribes aureum* var. *villosum*. It is native to central USA, has lax branches that are covered in striking, golden-yellow, star-like flowers (from where it gets its other common name, the golden currant), with darker central bosses of stamens. Its flowers have a wonderful spicy, clove-like scent. They are followed by spherical black fruits.

The foliage is also scented with leaves that are three- or five-lobed, turning red and purple in autumn.

Prune it annually after flowering, removing some of the oldest stems and branches down to ground level.

ASPECT: Full sun to partial shade.
FLOWERING: March–April.
SCENT: Medium.
HARDINESS: -10 to -15 °C (14 to 5 °F).

1.5–2 m (5–7 ft)
1.5–2 m (5–7 ft)

SAMBUCUS NIGRA
Common elder
VIBURNACEAE

The common elder is a very pretty and ornamental-looking deciduous shrub that will develop into a smallish tree if left unpruned, but this will mean that most of the flowers will be produced at a high level, which is not ideal. Mature specimens have attractive, corky bark. Its foliage is also attractive, with some varieties like **'Black Lace'** having very dark and finely cut leaves. The flowers are flat-topped inflorescences made up of many tiny white flowers (pink-flushed in the case of 'Black Lace') that have a strong, distinctive scent. Some love it and some definitely don't!

The flowers are followed by small, shiny, black elderberries. Both the flowers and berries are used to make wine or cordials.

Pruning annually in spring will not only help keep a better-shaped shrub but will also produce younger stems, which will have better colour and flowers.

ASPECT: Full sun to partial shade.
FLOWERING: May–July.

Sambucus 'Black Lace'

SCENT: Medium
HARDINESS: -10 to -15 °C (14 to 5°F).

3–6 m (10–20 ft)
2.5–4 m (8–13 ft)

Ribes odoratum

Sambucus nigra

SHRUBS 107

Roses

Roses almost need no introduction, as they are one of the most recognisable of all garden plants and surely no scented garden would be complete without a rose or two!

So great is their range of types, colours and fragrances that there have been many books written about them. They are often referred to as the queen of flowers and the heady scent many of them produce is a smell of summer, while some continue to give autumn and winter interest with a variety of coloured hips.

Roses have been grown and valued for their fragrance for centuries. A garden favourite since the time of the Ancient Greeks, their cultivation also goes back centuries in China, where varieties were first developed through selection and hybridisation, before finding their way into Europe. These were crossed with the European cultivars in the 19th century, leading to the huge range we enjoy in our gardens today. Many of these old roses are known as Heritage roses, or Old Garden roses, and still survive today, such as the fragrant *Rosa gallica* 'Officinalis'.

Roses do really well when planted in a mixed border with other shrubs or as specimen plants in a herbaceous planting. The classic combinations are red roses with the blue flowers of salvias, or catmints, and paler pink ones with lavenders.

With such a huge range I only mention a few here, covering some of the most fragrant and popular, including choices for differing garden situations.

Roses are best pruned in their dormant season.

Prominent golden stamens shine out centrally from the pure white, sweetly scented, elegant blooms

Rosa 'Alba Semiplena'

Once flowering:

ROSA × ALBA 'ALBA SEMIPLENA' – A beautifully scented, semi-double rose, with pure white flowers borne on an arching stem in terminal clusters of up to 15 individual blooms. Each has a centre filled with golden yellow stamens. The flowers are followed by pretty scarlet hips. June–July. 2.5 x 1.5 m (8 x 5 ft).

ROSA × CENTIFOLIA – This is also known as the cabbage rose, due to the shape of the flowers, which are goblet-shaped and full of petals. Fortunately its scent bears no resemblance to cabbage! Its rosy-pink blooms appear in midsummer and have a strong, sweet fragrance. While its origins are unknown, it is thought to be a cross between two old roses, the Damask rose and the Gallica rose. June–July. 1.5 x 1.5 m (5 x 5 ft).

ROSA MUNDI – An old rose that is a sport from *Rosa gallica* 'Officinalis' and has strikingly beautiful, fragrant flowers that are pink- and white-striped and semi-double. It forms a compact and bushy shrub that produces masses of flowers in early summer. June–July. 1.25 x 1.25 m (4 x 4 ft).

Rosa × centifolia

Rosa mundi

Repeat flowering:

ROSA 'CHARLES DARWIN' – A wonderfully fragrant rose with large, lemon-yellow blooms that fade to a creamy-white as they age. A citrusy scent matches well with its lemony colour. It stays relatively small and rounded. June–September. 1.2 x 1.5 m (4 x 5 ft).

ROSA 'FELICIA' – A very prolific and free-flowering, disease-resistant rose that produces large clusters of up to 30 small, double, pale pink blooms darkening to salmon-pink in their centres, with a strong fruity musk scent. June–September. 1.8 x 1.8 m (6 x 6 ft).

ROSA 'ROSERAIE DE L'HAŸ' – One of the best of the hybrid rugosa roses, producing a profusion of large, double, purple-crimson blooms with a wonderful scent throughout the summer. The flowers fade to a paler colour as they mature and the apple-green summer foliage turns yellow in the autumn. June–September. 2 x 2 m (7 x 7 ft).

Rosa 'Felicia'

ASPECT: Full sun to partial shade.
FLOWERING: Indicated individually.
SCENT: Medium–strong.
HARDINESS: -10 to -15 °C (14 to 5 °F).

Indicated indivually
Indicated indivually

Rosa 'Charles Darwin'

Rosa 'Roseraie de l'Haÿ'

SHRUBS 109

ROSA ROXBURGHII
Burr rose

ROSACEAE

This deciduous shrub rose is also known as the sweet chestnut rose or chestnut rose because of its distinctive fruits. But everything about this rose is distinctive, including the peeling bark along its mature stems, adding winter interest, and leaves that are produced from 10–18 pairs of small leaflets, giving them an almost fern-like appearance.

The pleasantly fragrant flowers are produced in early summer and are dark pink with a white centre, usually single, and like many of the single-flowered roses, much loved by bees. But there is also a double-flowered form that was the original introduction into Europe in the early 19th century, and probably a hybrid.

The flowers are followed by large, ovoid, apple-like fruits that are covered in small spines, similar to those of the sweet chestnut *Castanea sativa*. As the fruits ripen, they turn from green to yellow and are highly fragrant.

This is a rose best left unpruned, just removing the oldest wood low down, if necessary, in winter.

ASPECT: Full sun to partial shade.
FLOWERING: May–June.
SCENT: Strong.
HARDINESS: -10 to -15 °C (14 to 5 °F).

1.5–2 m (5–7 ft)
1.5–2 m (5–7 ft)

Rosa roxburghii

ROSA RUGOSA
Rugosa rose

ROSACEAE

The rugosa rose is easy to grow, disease-resistant, and not too fussy about its growing conditions. It is a vigorous rose with pink, fragrant flowers that are generally single with central golden stamens, but can occasionally have some semi-double flowers.

It has tough, prickly stems, and its habit to sucker makes it an ideal rose for growing as a fragrant, flowering hedge that will produce flowers from early summer until the autumn, when its foliage turns golden-yellow or bronze. The flowers are followed by reddish orange, round hips.

ASPECT: Full sun to partial shade.
FLOWERING: June–August.
SCENT: Strong.
HARDINESS: -10 to -15 °C (14 to 5 °F).

1.5–2 m (5–7 ft)
1.5–2 m (5–7 ft)

Rosa rugosa

Santolina chamaecyparissus

SANTOLINA CHAMAECYPARISSUS
Cotton lavender
ASTERACEAE

This is a pretty little evergreen shrub that is often referred to as dwarf, but in ideal conditions it can reach a height of up to 1 m. However, there is a dwarf cultivar called **'Nana'** that will remain more compact.

Despite being of Mediterranean origin, cotton lavender is fully hardy and forms a rounded, bushy plant with fine, silvery-grey, aromatic, deeply cut fern-like foliage. The small, bright yellow pompom or button-like flowers are borne in profusion and held above the foliage on individual slender stems. It makes an ideal plant for growing as a low hedge along the edge of a sunny border.

Annual pruning should be carried out after flowering, just below the flowering stems to prevent the plant becoming too woody. If grown as a hedge, trim regularly.

ASPECT: Full sun.
FLOWERING: June–August.
SCENT: Strong.
HARDINESS: -10 to -15 °C (14 to 5 °F).

50–75 cm (20–30 in)
50–75 m (20–30 in)

SARCOCOCCA CONFUSA
Christmas box
BUXACEAE

As its common name suggests, this medium-sized evergreen shrub flowers from late December – around Christmas time.

It has very dark green, shiny foliage that shows off the highly fragrant, creamy-white flowers with their protruding stamens. The flowers are borne in profusion in small clusters in the leaf axils, covering much of the plant. Glossy black berries are produced from the flowers, and it is common to have both at the same time.

Being very tolerant of deep shade makes this plant ideal for brightening up a gloomy spot.

Sarcococca confusa

Minimal pruning is needed. Prune after flowering, removing any damaged material but keeping the plant's natural habit.
ASPECT: Full sun to partial shade.
FLOWERING: December–March.
SCENT: Strong.
HARDINESS: -10 to -15 °C (14 to 5 °F).

1–1.5 m (3–5 ft)
1–1.5 m (3–5 ft)

SARCOCOCCA HOOKERIANA VAR. DIGYNA
Sweet box
BUXACEAE

A plant similar to *Sarcococca confusa* (see above), sweet box is an evergreen, medium-sized shrub that produces clusters of creamy-white, fragrant flowers. However, the flowers differ in that they have pinkish-red colouring at the base of the stamens, and they are borne along purplish stems. The foliage also differs – the dark green leaves are longer and narrower. Glossy black berries follow flowering.

Sarcococca hookeriana var. digyna

Like *Sarcococca confusa*, this shrub will tolerate deep shade.

Minimal pruning is needed. Prune after flowering, removing any damaged material but keeping the plant's natural habit.

ASPECT: Full sun to partial shade.
FLOWERING: October–March.
SCENT: Strong.
HARDINESS: -10 to -15 °C (14 to 5 °F).

1–1.5 m (3–5 ft)
1–1.5 m (3–5 ft)

SKIMMIA × CONFUSA 'KEW GREEN'
Skimmia
RUTACEAE

This is a compact, dome-shaped, evergreen shrub that will tolerate a shady spot in the garden as long as it gets a few hours of sun each day. It produces tight green buds in winter that open to create terminal, dense clusters of creamy-white, fragrant flowers that are set off well against the dark green, glossy foliage. The flowers open over a period of several weeks.

This is a male clone so will not produce berries after flowering, but is needed for female varieties like **'Kew White'**, which produces creamy-white berries, and *Skimmia japonica* 'Nymans', which has shiny red berries.

Any necessary pruning should be carried out after flowering.

ASPECT: Full sun to partial shade.
FLOWERING: April–May.
SCENT: Medium.
HARDINESS: -10 to -15 °C (14 to 5 °F).

0.5–1 m (20 in–3 ft)
1–1.5 m (3–5 ft)

SKIMMIA JAPONICA 'FRAGRANT CLOUD'
Skimmia 'Fragrant Cloud'
RUTACEAE

The cultivar 'Fragrant Cloud' is a male form of skimmia so only produces flowers and not berries, but it is the fragrant flowers that are the main feature of this small evergreen shrub.

During the winter months the buds form to give winter interest, contrasting well against the glossy, dark green foliage, and then in late spring this dome-shaped shrub opens large flowerheads of creamy-white flowers that have an attractive scent, similar to lily of the valley.

It is a fairly low-maintenance shrub requiring very little pruning. Any pruning that is carried out should be done in late spring after flowering.

ASPECT: Full sun to partial shade.
FLOWERING: April–May.
SCENT: Medium.
HARDINESS: -10 to -15 °C (14 to 5 °F).

0.5–1 m (20 in–3 ft)
1–1.5 m (3–5 ft)

SPARTIUM JUNCEUM
Spanish broom
FABACEAE

Spanish broom is a tall deciduous shrub that is green all year round, for a short period it just has very few small leaves covered in silky hairs on the undersides. Its round, rush-like stems are dark green and throughout the summer months are transformed by a profusion of colour. Large golden-yellow, fragrant, pea-like flowers cover the upper parts of this plant in long arching terminal racemes.

It can be a difficult plant to place in a garden because it is fast-growing and can become a bit straggly and bare around the base, although it can be pruned hard every few years to keep it tidy and in check.

General pruning should be carried out after flowering has finished.

ASPECT: Full sun.
FLOWERING: June–September.
SCENT: Medium.
HARDINESS: -10 to -15 °C (14 to 5 °F).

2–3 m (7–10 ft)
1.5–2.5 m (5–8 ft)

Skimmia × *confusa* 'Kew Green'

Spartium junceum

SYRINGA LACINIATA
Feathered Persian lilac
OLEACEAE

There is some debate as to the correct name of this plant. It can be found under the names *Syringa persica* and *Syringa* x *Persica* var. *laciniata*, as well as another common name, the cut-leaf lilac.

But what is not disputed is the fact that this medium-sized deciduous shrub has wonderful fragrance.

It is the perfect shrub for a small garden, with its rounded habit making it suitable for beds, borders, or as a standalone specimen that will produce masses of small, pale lilac or purple, trumpet-like flowers in spring.

The only pruning that is necessary is light pruning or shaping after flowering in late spring or early summer.

ASPECT: Full sun.
FLOWERING: April–May.
SCENT: Medium.
HARDINESS: -10 to -15 °C (14 to 5 °F).

2 m (7 ft)
1.5–2 m (5–7 ft)

SYRINGA MEYERI
Korean lilac
OLEACEAE

This is another great medium-sized fragrant shrub for a small garden, but it will do equally well in a garden of any size.

Similar in size to the Persian lilac (see above), it makes a small, rounded, slow-growing deciduous shrub with flower spikes made up of dozens of small, fragrant, lilac or pink flowers that contrast well against the dark green leaves.

A pre-1920 cultivar of unknown origin is named **'Palibin'** and is particularly small, growing to around 1.5 m (5 ft) when fully mature. Its flowers are pinkish, opening from deep purple buds.

Very little if any pruning is needed but should be carried out in late spring after flowering.

ASPECT: Full sun.
FLOWERING: April–June.
SCENT: Medium.
HARDINESS: -10 to -15 °C (14 to 5 °F).

2–3 m (7–10 ft)
1.5–2.5 m (5–8 ft)

Syringa laciniata

Syringa meyeri

SHRUBS 113

Syringa tomentella subsp. *yunnanensis*

SYRINGA TOMENTELLA SUBSP. YUNNANENSIS
Yunnan lilac
OLEACEAE

The Yunnan lilac is a large deciduous shrub or small tree with an erect, loose, open habit, with large oval-shaped dull green leaves.

The fragrant, small white or pinkish-white, trumpet-shaped fragrant flowers are borne in loosely branched, terminal clusters.

This is a large lilac that should be planted where it can be given room to grow to maturity, so that it can keep its natural shape. Little pruning would then be needed apart from some stem removal of the oldest wood if necessary, which should be carried out after flowering.
ASPECT: Full sun to partial shade.
FLOWERING: May–July.
SCENT: Medium.
HARDINESS: -10 to -15 °C (14 to 5 °F).

3–5 m (10–16 ft)
2.5–4 m (8–13 ft)

SYRINGA VULGARIS
Common lilac
OLEACEAE

This wonderful species is a large and vigorous deciduous shrub that has been bred into a wealth of modern varieties. Many have the rich-scented flowers that are characteristic of the species, but some of the modern cultivars do not have the same strong fragrance, although all are fragrant to differing degrees. The flowers are both single and double (singles definitely have the edge on fragrance), in a wide range of colours. There are thought to be well over a thousand different named selections going back to the late-19th and early-20th century.

There are many other species of *Syringa*, but none can equal that of the common lilac, *Syringa vulgaris*, for the range of cultivars. Many of these are very similar, however, with few distinctions, and with the ever-changing fashions in gardening, lilacs are less popular today than they were a few decades ago. But this is a must-have shrub in a garden where early-season scent is key.

With these changing garden fashions the availability of named cultivars is also ever-changing, so below is just a selection showing the available colour range of both single- and double-flowered forms.

Singles:

'ANNA NICKELS' has spikes of well-scented flowers that are the classic lilac/purple colour, with the darker purple buds opening to lilac. 2–3 m x 2 m (6–10 ft x 6 ft).

'HEAVENLY BLUE' as the name suggests has beautiful spikes of pale blue flowers which open from plum-coloured buds. 3 m x 3 m (10 ft x 10 ft).

'MONUMENT' produces pure white, sweetly scented flowers from creamy-greenish buds. 3 m x 3 m (10 ft x 10 ft).

'SENSATION' is a very distinctive lilac with large trusses of rich purple, single flowers, each with a white margin to its petals, and a sweet scent. 4 m x 3 m (13 x 10 ft).

Doubles:

'JOAN DUNBAR' with its pure white, scented double flowers has an almost bubbly appearance. As with 'Monument' the flowers open from creamy or pale green buds. 3 m x 3 m (10 ft x 10 ft).

'NADEZHDA' has spectacularly large clusters of fragrant, lavender-coloured, double flowers. A Russian hybrid bred to have longer-lasting flowers. 3 m x 3 m (10 ft x 10 ft).

Syringa vulgaris 'Anna Nickels'

'LE NOTRE' has large individual flowers that are deep pink in bud, opening to violet-purple. This is an old cultivar dating to 1922. 3 m x 2 m (10 ft x 6 ft).

'MADAME ANTOINE BUCHNER' is a very popular cultivar with pale pink, strongly scented double flowers that open from deep red buds. 4 m x 4 m (13 ft x 13 ft).

Pruning should be left until the shrub has reached your desired height and spread, then carried out immediately after flowering back to a strong pair of buds below the spent flower spike.

ASPECT: Full sun to partial shade.
FLOWERING: April–June.
SCENT: Strong.
HARDINESS: -10 to -15 °C (14 to 5 °F).

2.5–3 m (8–10 ft)
2.5–3 m (8–10 ft)

Syringa vulgaris 'Heavenly Blue'

Syringa vulgaris 'Sensation'

Syringa vulgaris 'Monument'

Syringa vulgaris 'Joan Dunbar'

SHRUBS

A very hardy old cultivar of the common lilac with wonderfully fragrant double flowers

Syringa vulgaris 'Le Notre'

Syringa vulgaris 'Nazedha'

Syringa vulgaris 'Madame Antoine Buchner'

SYRINGA × HYACINTHIFLORA
Early flowering hybrid lilac
OLEACEAE

These lilacs have been raised by the crossing of two species, *Syringa oblata* and *Syringa vulgaris*, mainly to produce larger, earlier flowering blooms with a good scent. Like both parents, they are deciduous.

'Esther Staley' is a large, bushy shrub with upright spikes of lilac-pink single flowers opening from reddish buds. The large flowers tend to droop when fully open. 4 m x 3 m (13 ft x 10 ft).

'The Bride' has large white spikes of flowers that stand out well against the dark green foliage of this large, upright shrub. 4 m x 4 m (13 ft x 13 ft).

'Turgot' is one of the first into flower, producing beautiful rosy-pink, single flowers from deeper pink buds. 3 m x 3 m (10 ft x 10 ft).

ASPECT: Full sun to partial shade.
FLOWERING: April–May.
SCENT: Strong.
HARDINESS: -10 to -15 °C (14 to 5 °F).

2.5–3 m (8–10 ft)
2.5–3 m (8–10 ft)

Syringa × hyacinthiflora 'The Bride'

ULEX EUROPAEUS
Common gorse
FABACEAE

This evergreen, upright, rounded shrub is a bit of a prickly customer. It has very sharp, spine-tipped green stems. Its leaves are also long and sharp. The flowers are a vibrant yellow and pea-like, and cover most of the plant when it is in full flower. They have a distinct coconut scent.

The flowers are followed by hairy pods that open with an audible crack in hot weather.

There is also a semi-double flowered form named 'Flore Pleno' that is more compact, growing to 1.5 m (5 ft) tall.

If you have an area in the garden set aside for wildlife, then this an ideal plant. It's loved by bees and provides a safe and secure nesting site for many small garden birds.

Syringa × hyacinthiflora 'Esther Staley'

Syringa × hyacinthiflora 'Turgot'

Ulex europaeus

Pruning is best carried out after flowering, but it needs very little, apart from removing any dead or damaged branches. A robust pair of gloves should be used when tackling this plant.
ASPECT: Full sun to partial shade.
FLOWERING: February–May.
SCENT: Strong.
HARDINESS: -10 to -15 °C (14 to 5 °F).

1.5–2.5 m (5–8 ft)
1.5–2 m (5–7 ft)

VIBURNUM × BODNANTENSE
Bodnant viburnum
VIBURNACEAE

This deciduous shrub is a cross between *Viburnum farreri* and *Viburnum grandiflorum* and makes a large, woody plant with upright stems.

The new young foliage, which is produced in spring, is an attractive bronze colour, turning green with age. But it is the flowers that are the star of this plant. It has a long flowering period, producing clusters of pink, trumpet-shaped, strongly scented flowers borne on the bare wood from late autumn through until spring.

This cross has also produced some award-winning cultivars.

Viburnum × bodnantense

Viburnum × carlcephalum

'Charles Lamont' has pale pink flowers.

'Dawn' is probably the most popular and famous selection, with clusters of white flowers tinged with pink, opening from reddish buds.

'Deben' is the whitest of the three cultivars, opening from pink buds.

Prune out older stems from the base every few years to make way for younger, more productive growth to maintain a good show of flowers.
ASPECT: Full sun to partial shade.
FLOWERING: February–May.
SCENT: Strong.
HARDINESS: -10 to -15 °C (14 to 5 °F).

2–4 m (7–13 ft)
1.5–2.5 m (5–8 ft)

VIBURNUM × CARLCEPHALUM
Fragrant snowball
VIBURNACEAE

This is a large, rounded and bushy deciduous shrub that produces large, snowball-like inflorescences that are packed with small waxy flowers. These are highly fragrant, similar to those of one of its parents *Viburnum carlesii* (see below). It gets its rounded flower shape from its nonfragrant parent, *Viburnum macrocephalum*.

The flowers in each cluster open over a short period, so that you have both pink buds and open white flowers at the same time, but eventually they are all fully open. The flowers are followed by shiny red, oval, inedible fruits.

This plant also has the added bonus of providing good autumn colour.

Very little pruning is necessary, other than the removal of dead or damaged growth, and should be carried out in late spring after flowering.
ASPECT: Full sun to partial shade.
FLOWERING: March–May.
SCENT: Strong.
HARDINESS: - 10 to -15 °C (14 to 5 °F).

1.5–2 m (5–7 ft)
1.5–2 m (5–7 ft)

Viburnum carlesii

Viburnum farreri

VIBURNUM CARLESII
Korean spice viburnum
VIBURNACEAE

This medium-sized shrub is ideal for most gardens as it is slow-growing, doesn't get too big and has year-round interest.

It flowers from early spring, producing tight, rounded clusters of ball-shaped, white, or pinkish-white flowers with a rich heady fragrance that fills the air around the plant. It has good red autumnal colour, and jet-black fruits.

The cultivar **'Aurora'** is red in bud, with flowers opening pink.

Very little pruning is necessary, other than the removal of dead or damaged growth, and should be carried out in late spring after flowering.

ASPECT: Full sun to partial shade.
FLOWERING: March–May.
SCENT: Strong.
HARDINESS: -10 to -15 °C (14 to 5 °F).

1.5–2 m (5–7 ft)
1.5–2 m (5–7 ft)

VIBURNUM FARRERI
Farrer viburnum
VIBURNACEAE

This viburnum is deciduous and has an upright habit when young, becoming more rounded with age. Its flowers – which are produced from late autumn – are variable in colour, from pinkish white to almost pure white.

The flowers are borne on its bare branches in large clusters and are highly fragrant. The new foliage opens bronze in spring with the last of the flowers, turning darker green, with pronounced parallel veins as it matures.

To maintain a good show of flowers, prune out older stems from the base every few years to make way for younger, more productive growth.

ASPECT: Full sun to partial shade.
FLOWERING: November–March.
SCENT: Strong.
HARDINESS: -10 to -15 °C (14 to 5 °F).

1.5–2.5 m (5–8 ft)
1.5–2 m (5–7 ft)

VIBURNUM TINUS 'LUCIDUM'
Laurustinus 'Lucidum'
VIBURNACEAE

Viburnum tinus has always been a favourite evergreen shrub of mine and particularly so after I saw it growing in the wild in southern Spain and realised what a tough plant it is – tolerant of drought and poor soils. But what I had never associated it with was fragrance. That was until I came across the cultivar 'Lucidum'.

Viburnum tinus 'Lucidum'

It is quite different from the type species with much larger, oval, glossy leaves and larger heads of creamy-white flowers that bloom a little later than the species. Like those of the species, the flowers are often followed by iridescent, blue-black berries.

Only light pruning needs to be carried out, apart from removing any dead, dying and diseased material, and this should be done in late spring after flowering.

ASPECT: Full sun to partial shade.
FLOWERING: December–March.
SCENT: Strong.
HARDINESS: -10 to -15 °C (14 to 5 °F).

1.5–2.5 m (5–8 ft)
1.5–2 m (5–7 ft)

Vitex agnus-castus

VITEX AGNUS-CASTUS
Chaste tree
LAMIACEAE

This is a large deciduous shrub with an open, spreading habit that is native to the Mediterranean region. In ideal conditions it will grow to make a small tree, but it is most commonly grown as a shrub.

Both its foliage and flowers are fragrant. Its attractive, aromatic leaves are palmate and made up of five or seven long, narrow leaflets. The fragrant, lilac-coloured flowers are borne on long terminal spikes in late summer, looking similar to those of buddleja.

To get the best flowering it needs to be grown in full sun and it does particularly well when grown as a wall shrub on a warm and sunny south-facing wall or fence.

The seeds of the chaste tree have been used in herbal medicine for centuries to treat gynaecological issues and it is still a common herbal medicine today. However, seeds are only produced in very hot summers in the UK.

The flowers are produced on the current year's growth so pruning should be carried out annually in spring, and older plants can be hard pruned to encourage young flowering stems.

ASPECT: Full sun to partial shade.
FLOWERING: August–October.
SCENT: Light.
HARDINESS: -5 to -10 °C (23 to 14 °F).

1.5–2.5 m (5–8 ft)
1.5–2 m (5–7 ft)

ZABELIA TRIFLORA
Three-flowered zabelia
CAPRIFOLIACEAE

This is a large deciduous shrub with a graceful habit. It is a plant that is rarely seen in gardens, but for the rich sweet scent of the flowers alone it is one that should be more commonly grown.

The leaves are dark green and lance-shaped, above which their tubular, white,

Zabelia triflora

sometimes pink-tinged, star-like flowers are borne in dense, terminal clusters.

Little or no pruning is needed with this shrub. If it gets very congested some of the older wood can be removed down to the base, which will encourage younger shots to develop.

ASPECT: Full sun to partial shade.
FLOWERING: June–July.
SCENT: Strong.
HARDINESS: -10 to -15 °C (14 to 5 °F).

2.5–5 m (8–16 ft)
1.5–2.5 m (5–8 ft)

YUCCA FILAMENTOSA
Adam's needle
ASPARAGACEAE

This is truly a statement plant, producing towering flowering spikes of large, creamy-white, bell-shaped, nodding flowers that are wonderfully lemon-scented. It produces suckers that will continue its flowering year after year.

There is also a variety called **'Bright Edge'** that has golden-yellow leaf margins and usually grows to around 1.5 m (5 ft) tall.

This stunning architectural plant comes with a health warning. The dark green, evergreen basal rosettes of sword-like leaves have very sharp pointed tips and serrated leaf edges, so this should be borne in mind when choosing its planting position. It's an ideal specimen plant for a sunny gravel bed and looks great planted in a small group.

Faded flowering spikes should be removed at the end of the season.

ASPECT: Full sun.
FLOWERING: June–August.
SCENT: Medium.
HARDINESS: -10 to -15 °C (14 to 5 °F).

1.5–2 m (5–7 ft)
1.5–2 m (5–7 ft)

Yucca filamentosa

ZENOBIA PULVERULENTA
Honeycups
ERICACEAE

Zenobia pulverulenta is not a commonly grown small shrub. The flowers are reminiscent of the bell-shaped flowers of the woodland bulb, lily of the valley. They are, though, in completely different families.

Honeycups is semi-evergreen in most winters but will lose its leaves in the coldest winters. The leaves are glaucous, blue-green when young, maturing to a darker green, and with good autumn colour when grown in a sunny site. The fragrant, bell-shaped white flowers are occasionally flushed with pink and borne on arching stems in small clusters. They have an aniseed scent.

Being in the Ericaceae family, it needs to be grown in acidic soil with a pH lower than 7, ideally around pH 6, so if rhododendrons do well in your garden,

Zenobia pulverulenta

then so will this pretty little shrub, which is native to the open woodlands of eastern America. But it will also do well grown in a container with ericaceous compost.

Pruning is minimal and should be carried out after flowering, as flowers are produced on the previous year's growth.

ASPECT: Partial shade to full sun.
FLOWERING: June–July.
SCENT: Medium.
HARDINESS: -10 to -15 °C (14 to 5 °F).

1–1.5 m (3–5 ft)
1–1.5 m (3–5 ft)

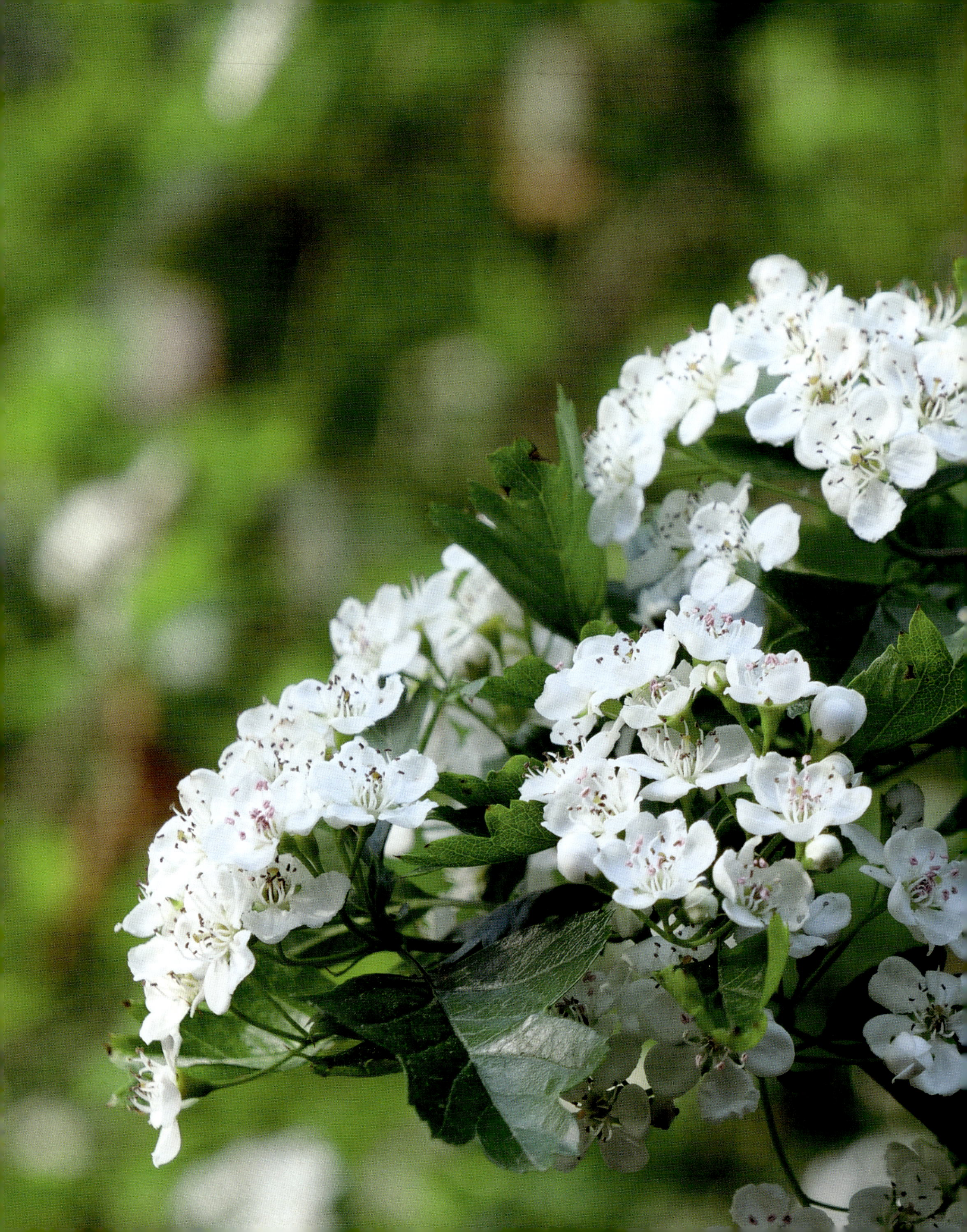

Trees

ACACIA DEALBATA
Blue wattle
FABACEAE

This is a fast-growing evergreen tree native to Australia that will tolerate a few degrees of frost but needs a bit of protection from cold winds. It has proved to be hardy in the south of England. Commonly called the blue wattle, like many of the wattles it has attractive, silvery-green, fern-like foliage.

From late winter through until early spring, it produces bright yellow, fluffy, pompom-like fragrant flowers. It will flower best in an open but sheltered, sunny spot.

It has very pliable wood and was used by the early European settlers in Australia for wattle and daub in their buildings, from where it gets its common name.

It does not like hard pruning, so a light prune can be carried out after flowering in late spring if needed, removing any frosted or dead wood.

ASPECT: Full sun to partial shade.
FLOWERING: February–April.
SCENT: Medium.
HARDINESS: 1 to -5 °C (34 to 23 °F).

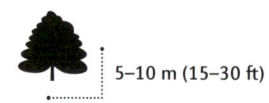

5–10 m (15–30 ft)
4–6 m (5–20 ft)

ALBIZIA JULIBRISSIN
Persian silk tree
FABACEAE

Albizia is an attractive, deciduous, small, spreading tree that has the most amazing, exotic-looking flowers. They are borne in mid- to late summer and sit boldly above their feather-like, twice-pinnate foliage, which is made up of many tiny crescent-shaped leaflets, along drooping branches.

The unusual-looking flowers are a real feature, being produced in clusters of fluffy pink blooms with prominent,

Acacia dealbata

pinkish-red stamens that become paler towards their base.

Albizia julibrissin **'Summer Chocolate'** is a cultivar with dark purple foliage and the same attractive flowers.

Any pruning needed to restrict growth should be done during the spring, cutting back the previous year's growth. This is a small tree that will definitely be a talking point.

ASPECT: Full sun.
FLOWERING: June–August.
SCENT: Light.
HARDINESS: -5 to -10 °C (23 to 14 °F).

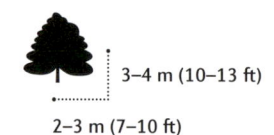

3–4 m (10–13 ft)
2–3 m (7–10 ft)

CALOCEDRUS DECURRENS
Incense cedar
CUPRESSACEAE

This is a tall conifer with a narrow, pyramidal habit. It is most suited to a larger garden but its upright habit also makes it a good screening tree in any moderate-sized garden if space is limited, where it will provide height without becoming too wide. It can also be clipped from a young age and treated as a medium-sized hedge.

The attractive, soft, dark green, evergreen fern-like foliage is strongly aromatic when rubbed. Its trunk becomes cracked and peeling with age and its lower branches should be lifted to show this off if grown as a single specimen.

As a native of California, it is relatively drought-tolerant once established.

Albizia julibrissin

Calocedrus decurrens

Catalpa ovata

Cercidiphyllum japonicum

   No pruning should be necessary, unless it is growing as a hedge, in which case it can be clipped once a year in late spring or early autumn.
ASPECT: Full sun to partial shade.
SCENTED FOLIAGE: Strong.
HARDINESS: -5 to -10 °C (23 to 14 °F).

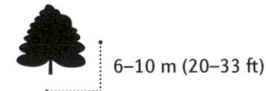

6–10 m (20–33 ft)
2.5–4 m (8–10 ft)

CATALPA OVATA
Yellow catalpa
BIGNONIACEAE
This large deciduous tree has a spreading crown with very large, heart-shaped leaves with three- or five-pointed lobes, covered with soft hairs on their undersides. Catalpas are quite late coming into leaf, usually in late spring.
   Clusters of around 15 individual creamy-white or yellow flowers, which are bell-shaped with reddish spotting inside and darker yellow blotches on their lobes, are borne in terminal panicles, forming a loose pyramidal shape. The flowers are followed by clusters of long, pencil-thin, pointed seed pods.
   Because of its size, this is really a tree for bigger gardens, where it can be given room to mature.
   Pruning should be minimal, removing any new growth damaged by late frosts, after all risk of frost has passed.
ASPECT: Full sun to partial shade.
FLOWERING: July–August.
SCENT: Medium.
HARDINESS: 1 to -5 °C (34 to 23 °F).

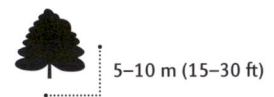

5–10 m (15–30 ft)
4–6 m (13–20 ft)

CERCIDIPHYLLUM JAPONICUM
Katsura tree
CERCIDIPHYLLACEAE
This is one of my favourite small- to medium-sized trees, and it's all about the foliage – its scent and colour changes throughout the seasons.
   The most common form for this small tree is growing as a standard on a single stem, but I much prefer to see it grown as a multi-stemmed form, branching from low down.
   New heart-shaped leaves emerge in spring with subtle coppery or pinkish tones, changing to a dull green as they progress into summer. But it is as they start to go into autumn that they put on a superb show as their foliage turns shades of yellow, orange, pink, purple and red, and they fill the air for some distance around with the scent of caramel and candyfloss.
   No pruning is necessary apart from removing dead, damaged or diseased branches.
ASPECT: Full sun to partial shade.
FLOWERING: Inconspicuous.
SCENTED FOLIAGE: Strong.
HARDINESS: - 5 to -10 °C (23 to 14 °F).

4–12 m (13–39 ft)
4–8 m (13–26 ft)

TREES 125

Chionanthus retusus

Chionanthus retusus flower

CHIONANTHUS RETUSUS
Chinese fringe tree
OLEACEAE

This is a small, deciduous tree that is often grown as a large shrub. Once mature it has wonderful deeply fissured and peeling cinnamon-coloured bark on both the trunk and branches.

Its bright green leaves are the perfect contrast for its white, fringe-like, fragrant flowers, which are spectacular when in full bloom and covering the whole tree.

This is an androdioecious species, meaning that some individuals have only male flowers, while others have hermaphrodite flowers.

It needs little or no pruning, apart from removing dead, damaged or diseased wood.

ASPECT: Full sun.
FLOWERING: June–July.
SCENT: Medium.
HARDINESS: -5 to -10 °C (23 to 14 °F).

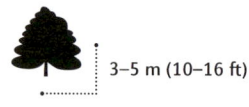

3–5 m (10–16 ft)
2–4 m (6.5–13 ft)

CORDYLINE AUSTRALIS
New Zealand cabbage palm
ASPARAGACEAE

Strictly speaking this is not a tree, but a branched monocot, and very palm-like.

It has common names that include cabbage tree, and in Britain it is also known as the Torbay or Cornish palm, as it is a very familiar sight in many gardens and even as a street tree in the southwest of the country, growing very well in coastal areas.

This exotic-looking plant produces a palm-like trunk, with a head of long, sword-shaped evergreen leaves. Branching usually occurs once it has flowered and then it becomes more tree-like.

The small white flowers are strongly fragrant and borne in huge flowering spikes that contain hundreds of individual flowers.

It's not usually pruned, but as the trunks grow in height remove lower dead leaves with secateurs.

ASPECT: Full sun to partial shade.
FLOWERING: June–August.
SCENT: Strong.
HARDINESS: -5 to -10 °C (23 to 14 °F).

Cordyline australis

5–6 m (16–20 ft)
2–3 m (7–10 ft)

CITRUS SPECIES AND HYBRIDS
RUTACEAE

Most citrus are not fully hardy, and I include them because of their fragrant flowers, leaves and fragrant fruits. Most of the different types will make small trees. All are evergreen.

They are most often bought as half standards for container growing.

They are great plants for growing in large containers and pots, where they can be placed out in garden positions throughout the summer to enjoy the extra light, and then given some protection during the winter in a conservatory or frost-free greenhouse, as they need to be kept cool not hot during this period.

They all have white, five-petalled, star-like, highly fragrant flowers that bloom on and off from late winter until autumn and will often have both flower and ripe fruit at the same time.

I have only listed the three most common – there are many more.

CITRUS × *AURANTIUM* F. *AURANTIUM* – known as the Mediterranean sweet orange, it also has the synonym *Citrus* × *sinensis*.

CITRUS × *LIMON* – Lemon.

CITRUS RETICULATA – Mandarin.

Most citrus require only minimal pruning to retain a good shape, and this should be mostly carried out in late winter. Any subsequent water shoots that arise should be removed or shortened if necessary to improve the overall shape.

ASPECT: Full sun to partial shade.
FLOWERING: February–September (often all year round).
SCENT: Strong
HARDINESS: 1 to 5 °C (34 to 41 °F).

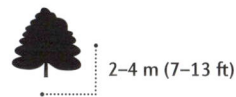

2–4 m (7–13 ft)
1–1.5 m (3–5 ft)

Citrus

CRATAEGUS MONOGYNA
Common hawthorn
ROSACEAE

This is also commonly known as the May tree, named for the season in which it usually flowers.

It's a small to medium-sized deciduous tree with deeply cut lobed leaves that also give good autumn colour, turning golden-yellow later in the year.

The scented, five-petalled, white or occasionally pink flowers are borne in flat-topped clusters along the tops of their branches, often covering the whole of the tree. They are very attractive to foraging and pollinating insects. The flowers are followed by red fruits known as 'haws'.

All parts of this tree are of value to wildlife, supporting over a hundred different species, and its thorny stems give good protection to nesting birds.

The common hawthorn is an ideal hedging plant, for both security and as part of a mixed native (UK) wildlife hedge.

Little or no pruning is necessary apart from removing dead, damaged or diseased wood.

ASPECT: Full sun to partial shade.
FLOWERING: April–May.
SCENT: Medium.
HARDINESS: -10 to -15 °C (14 to 5 °F).

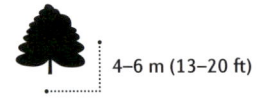

4–6 m (13–20 ft)
2–4 m (6.5–13 ft)

Crataegus monogyna

DRIMYS WINTERI
Winter's bark
WINTERACEAE

This is an evergreen, medium-sized tree or large shrub that has large, bright green leaves – with a silvery underside – that when crushed are aromatic.

It can be a bit ungainly, its branches becoming pendulous then hanging and

Drimys winteri

twisting around each other, giving the tree an untidy appearance. That said, it is a spectacular plant when in flower, as it is very floriferous, and flowers early in the year.

The flowers are fragrant, creamy-white and produced in large clusters of up to 20 and more blooms. The bark is also fragrant and was used to treat scurvy in the 16th century – it is now known to be rich in vitamin C.

This tree will benefit from the protection of a wall, preferably south-facing. Little or no pruning is required apart from in late spring to remove parts damaged during winter.

ASPECT: Partial shade–full sun.
FLOWERING: January–April.
SCENT: Not assessed.
HARDINESS: -5 to -10 °C (23 to 14°F).

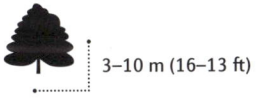

3–10 m (16–13 ft)
3–6 m (16–20 ft)

EHRETIA DICKSONII
BORAGINACEAE

This is a medium-sized, deciduous tree that is not commonly grown, but I think it should be, because once mature it is fully hardy and covered with clusters of fragrant white flowers and is a definite talking point in the garden. It will eventually grow up to around 6 m (20 ft) so it is best suited to a large garden where it can be given the space to grow to maturity.

The large green, leathery leaves are covered with stiff hairs, which is typical of plants in this family.

The clusters of fragrant, white, five-petalled flowers have protruding brown-tipped stamens, and stand out well above the foliage. They are often followed by yellow fruits that turn black when mature. Mature trees also have attractive corky, deeply fissured bark.

The less common *Ehretia acuminata* produces a small tree that is probably more floriferous and equally scented.

Young wood on this tree can sometimes be damaged in severe winters and should be pruned out during early summer when this damage will be evident against the new foliage.

ASPECT: Full sun to partial shade.
FLOWERING: May–June.
SCENT: Medium.
HARDINESS: -5 to -10 °C (23 to 14 °F).

5–8 m (16–26 ft)
4–5 m (13–16 ft)

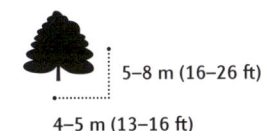

EMMENOPTERYS HENRYI
Henry's emmenopterys
RUBIACEAE

This is a tree that is still rare in cultivation, even though it was first introduced into the UK in 1907 by the well-known 20th century plant collector Ernest H. Wilson.

Emmenopterys henryi

It is even rarer to see it in flower as trees need to be mature and over 30 years of age before they will bloom. The first tree to flower in Britain was at Wakehurst Place in Sussex in 1987 when it was 75 years old.

It's a large deciduous tree with bronze-coloured young foliage, becoming mid-green in summer with pinkish-red petioles. Given time the tree will hopefully bear large clusters of creamy-white, fragrant flowers surrounded by white bracts.

The only pruning required is to remove any dead, dying or diseased wood.

ASPECT: Full sun.
FLOWERING: August–September.
SCENT: Medium.
HARDINESS: -5 to -10 °C (23 to 14 °F).

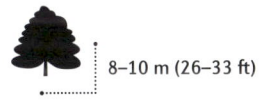

8–10 m (26–33 ft)
4–5 m (13–16 ft)

EUCALYPTUS SPECIES
Gum trees
MYRTACEAE

There are literally hundreds of eucalyptus species, the vast majority of them evergreen and native to Australia. They are particularly fast-growing and have aromatic, silvery or glaucous grey-green leaves and attractive, small fluffy flowers that are mainly white or cream, but also red. They are nectar-rich, attracting a range of pollinating insects.

Most eucalyptus are very ornamental, with attractive peeling bark, and the differing sizes of species will ensure that there will be one to fit most garden situations.

One of the best species for a small garden is *Eucalyptus pauciflora* subsp. *niphophila* which will grow to 4–5 m. But even the taller species like *Eucalyptus gunnii* can be cut back hard every year (coppiced) to produce new vibrant and aromatic foliage and keep the tree to a manageable height. But if left to grow to maturity, *E. gunnii* will easily reach 12 m tall, and some very much taller, but these are trees for arboretums and not regular gardens.

ASPECT: Full sun to partial shade.
FLOWERING: February–July.
SCENTED FOLIAGE: Strong.
HARDINESS: -5 to -10 °C (23 to 14 °F).

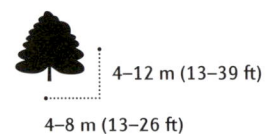

4–12 m (13–39 ft)
4–8 m (13–26 ft)

Eucalyptus

MAGNOLIA SPECIES
Magnolias
MAGNOLIACEAE

Magnolias are without doubt the most magnificent of all flowering trees and shrubs that are hardy in temperate regions, such as the UK. They have a range of flower colour from pure and creamy whites to pinks, purples and yellows. I have included those that are really shrubs here in order to keep them all together and describe their merits in one place.

As a general rule, the deciduous magnolias flower in the spring and the evergreen ones in the summer.

Their one downside is that the early-flowering ones can be caught out by a frost or cold winds, which can damage and discolour the flowers but will have little or no effect on the plants themselves.

There are also many different sizes, from those that will do well and can be grown in containers and small gardens, to much larger specimens more suited to a small woodland, so there is one to fit most situations.

MAGNOLIA DOLTSOPA, commonly known as the sweet Michelia, is a large evergreen tree that will grow up to 10 m (33 ft) tall in ideal conditions over a few decades. It has glossy green, leathery leaves that are glaucous on their undersides. The highly fragrant, large white flowers open from ginger-brown buds and fill the surrounding area with fragrance. Flowering: March to May. Hardiness: -5 to -10 °C (23 to 14 °F). Dimensions: 10 m x 6 m (33ft x 20 ft).

Magnolia doltsopa

Magnolia figo

TREES 131

MAGNOLIA FIGO is a great magnolia for a small garden. It produces a rounded shrub or small tree that will grow to around 4 m (13 ft) tall, with downy light brown stems and glossy dark green leaves. One of the common names for this plant is the banana magnolia because of the very strong, overripe banana-like scent produced by the flowers. These are small, pale yellow, with pale purple or red margins to the petals. Each flower only lasts a day or two, but they are produced in good numbers. Flowering: April to June. Hardiness: 1 to -5 °C (34 to 23 °F). Dimensions: 4 m x 2.5 m (13 ft x 8 ft).

MAGNOLIA GRANDIFLORA will make a large, rounded evergreen specimen tree that will grow to 8–10 m (26–33 ft), occasionally taller. It can also make a very good wall-trained specimen, should you have a wall tall enough to support it. It has large, glossy, dark green, oblong leaves, covered with a rusty-brown indumentum on their undersides. The large flowers are creamy-white, cup-shaped, highly fragrant, and around 25 cm (10 in) across. Flowering: August to September. Hardiness: -5 to -10 °C (23 to 14 °F). Dimensions: 10 m x 6 m (33 ft x 20 ft).

MAGNOLIA SIEBOLDII is commonly known as the Chinese magnolia and will eventually make a small tree. It has long, dark green leaves with a downy, glaucous underside and bears large saucer-shaped white flowers with a centre filled with showy crimson or purple stamens. If well pollinated during flowering, it will produce clusters of crimson fruits that split to reveal their orange-red seeds. Flowering: May to July. Hardiness: -10 to -15 °C (14 to 5 °F). Dimensions: 8 m x 4 m (26 ft x 13 ft).

Magnolia grandiflora

MAGNOLIA STELLATA is probably one of the best magnolias for growing in a small garden and is classed as a deciduous medium- to large-sized shrub. Known as the Star magnolia, this pretty plant develops a rounded habit and in early spring produces masses of pure white, star-shaped, fragrant flowers, which open from beautiful silky, soft buds. Its compact size also makes it an ideal plant for growing in a container. Flowering: March to April. Hardiness: -10 to -15 °C (14 to 5 °F). Dimensions: 3 m x 2.5 m (10 ft x 8 ft).

MAGNOLIA VIRGINIANA is deciduous or semi-evergreen, usually keeping its foliage in areas that have mild winters, but the plants themselves are fully hardy. The solitary, cup-shaped, creamy-white flowers are sweetly fragrant, hence one of its common names, the sweet bay magnolia. Each flower opens in the morning and closes again at night. Flowering: May to July. Hardiness: -10 to -15 °C (14 to 5 °F). Dimensions: 8 m x 3 m (26 ft x 10 ft).

Pruning of magnolias should be carried out after flowering while the plants are still actively growing.

ASPECT: Full sun to partial shade.
FLOWERING: Stated with each species.
SCENT: Light to strong.
HARDINESS: Stated with each species.

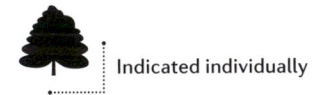

Indicated individually

Indicated individually

Magnolia stellata

Magnolia virginiana

TREES

Paulownia tomentosa

Prunus serrulata 'Jo-Nioi'

PAULOWNIA TOMENTOSA
Foxglove tree
PAULOWNIACEAE

The foxglove tree is a fast-growing deciduous tree that has large, heart-shaped, bright green leaves that are hairy on both surfaces. The gigantic leaves produced on young growth are one of this tree's main features, and to produce the biggest leaves (around 30 cm or 12 in across) it can be coppiced each year – although coppicing for the decorative leaves will be at the cost of the fragrant flowers, which are produced on wood grown in the previous year.

The flowers are lilac or pale purple and resemble those of the foxglove. They appear in terminal clusters, just before the leaves, on bare stems in late spring.

If pruning for foliage, cut back the stems to within 50–80 mm (2–3 in) of ground level in spring before growth starts.

The tree should also be pruned in spring to remove dead wood and any growth damaged by frost during cold winters.

ASPECT: Full sun.
FLOWERING: May–June.
SCENT: Light.
HARDINESS: -10 to -15 °C (14 to 5 °F).

8–10 m (26–33 ft)
5–7 m (16–23 ft)

PRUNUS SERRULATA 'JO-NIOI'
Cherry 'Jo-nioi'
ROSACEAE

This scented, flowering cherry has good interest throughout the seasons. In early spring, the new foliage emerges with pale golden-brown tints, just after the scented, white, single flowers have opened from pale pink buds. The flowers are borne individually on long hanging stalks in abundant terminal clusters.

Later in the season the leaves put on a show of autumn colour, turning orange and yellow.

No routine pruning is needed, apart from some formative pruning in young trees, which should be carried out in mid-summer allowing cuts to heal quickly, as the fungal disease silver leaf, *Chondrostereum pupureum*, which produces its spores in autumn and winter can be a potential problem for plants in the Rosaceae family.

ASPECT: Full sun.
FLOWERING: April–May.
SCENT: Medium.
HARDINESS: -10 to -15 °C (14 to 5 °F).

4–6 m (13–20 ft)
3–5 m (10–16 ft)

OPPOSITE
Prunus 'Shizuka' (see page 136)

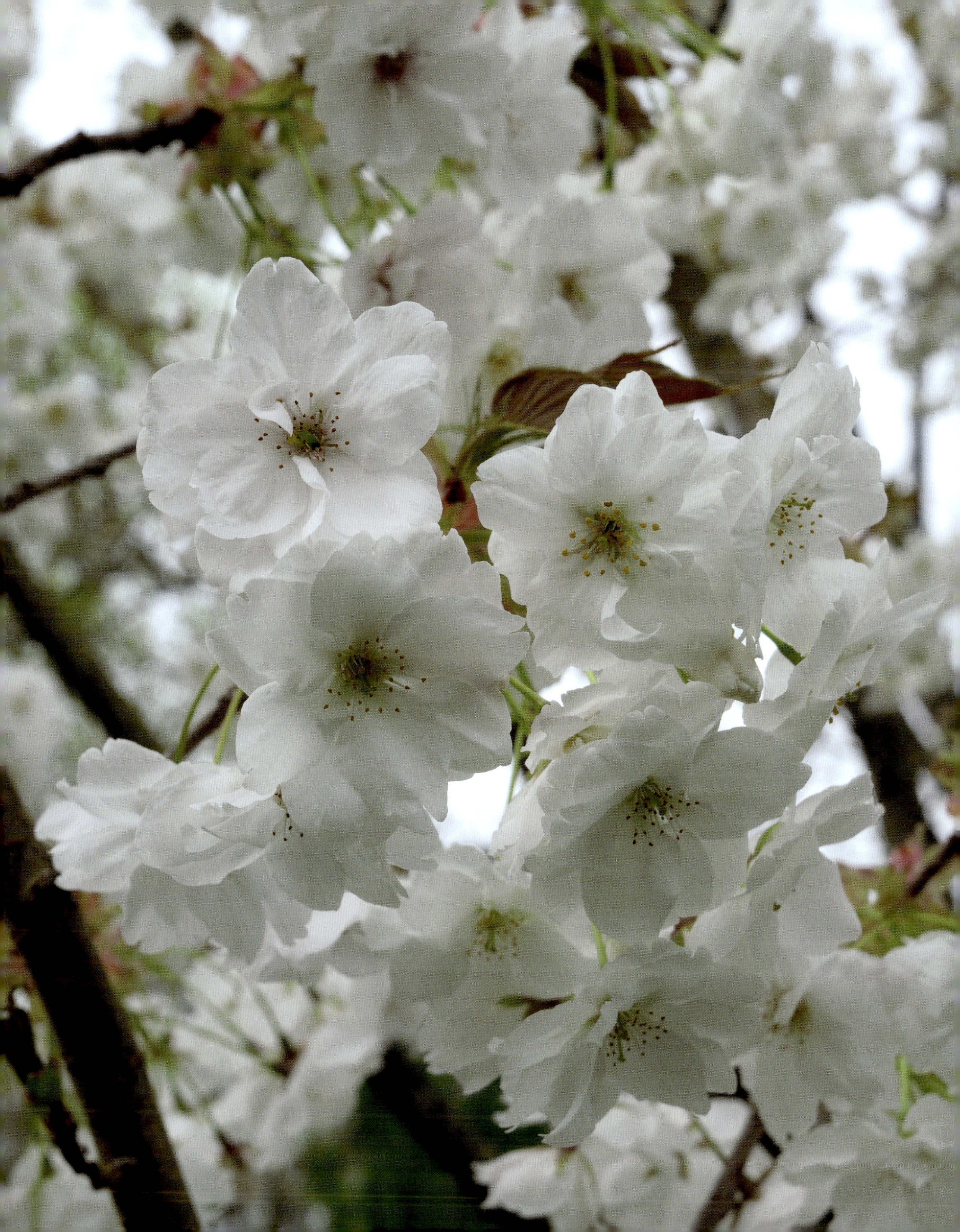

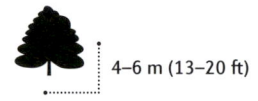

PRUNUS SERRULATA 'TAKI-NIOI'
Cherry 'Taki-nioi'
ROSACEAE

This is another of the scented cherries. The cultivar name, 'Taki-nioi', translates as 'fragrant waterfall', with *nioi* meaning fragrance and *taki* meaning waterfall in Japanese. Like Cherry 'Jo-nioi', it also has pure white single flowers, opening from pinkish buds, but they open a little later in the season, and the new leaves that emerge alongside the flowers have a rich, reddish-bronze tone.

Fragrant waterfall describes the plant well. When in full bloom the large clusters of flowers hang on lax branches resembling a waterfall.

Pruning advice is the same as for *Prunus serrulata* 'Jo-nioi' and should be carried out in mid-summer.

ASPECT: Full sun to partial shade.
FLOWERING: April–May.
SCENT: Medium.
HARDINESS: -10 to -15 °C (14 to 5 °F).

4–6 m (13–20 ft)
3–5 m (10–16 ft)

Prunus serrulata 'Taki-Nioi'

PRUNUS 'SHIZUKA'
Shizuka cherry
ROSACEAE

This pretty, semi-double flowered cherry is also known as Fragrant Cloud Shizuka. It is a relatively fast-growing, medium-sized tree with an upright habit.

The new leaves open a coppery bronze colour once the flowers are in bloom, turning darker green in early summer. The large, delightfully scented, decorative flowers open white, slowly maturing to a pale pink as they age, and are produced in large, massed clusters.

The Shizuka cherry also produces wonderful autumn colours, with the leaves turning a range of fiery oranges and reds before they fall.

Any pruning should be carried out in mid-summer to avoid the fungal spores of *Chondrostereum pupureum*, which are most active between autumn and winter and can cause the disease commonly known as silver leaf.

ASPECT: Full sun.
FLOWERING: April–May.
SCENT: Medium.
HARDINESS: -10 to -15 °C (14 to 5 °F).

4–6 m (13–20 ft)
3–4 m (10–13 ft)

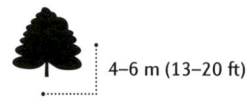

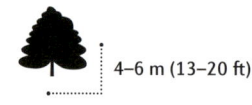

PRUNUS SPECIOSA
Oshima cherry
ROSACEAE

This medium-sized deciduous tree is named after the Japanese island of Oshima, where it is native. Like many cherries, the new foliage emerges bronze in colour, maturing to dark green from early summer. The overall shape of the tree is wide and spreading and it is very showy when in full flower.

The flowers are white, single and borne on individual stalks in small clusters from the leaf axils along the branches. They appear just before or around the same time as the new leaves emerge.

As with many of the cherries, this is a tree for all seasons. The flowers are followed by small black fruits and in autumn the leaves turn a mix of yellow and orange tones before they fall. Any pruning should be carried out in mid-summer to avoid the fungal spores of *Chondrostereum pupureum*, which are most active between autumn and winter and can cause the disease commonly known as silver leaf.

ASPECT: Full sun to partial shade.
FLOWERING: February–April.
SCENT: Medium.
HARDINESS: -10 to -15 °C (14 to 5 °F).

4–6 m (13–20 ft)
3–4 m (10–13 ft)

Prunus speciosa

Ptelea trifoliata

PTELEA TRIFOLIATA
Hop tree
RUTACEAE

This is a medium-sized deciduous tree that produces a rounded crown and has many seasons of interest. All parts of this distinctive tree are fragrant and aromatic.

The tree's unusual trifoliate leaves, from which it gets its specific epithet, are scented when crushed. Its bark is also aromatic, but it is the terminal clusters of small greenish-yellow flowers that produce the sweetest scent, similar to that of honeysuckle.

Once the flowers are over in late summer, decorative fruits are produced. They are flattened, winged discs, each encasing a single seed.

Any pruning should be carried out straight after flowering.

ASPECT: Full sun to partial shade.
FLOWERING: June–July.
SCENT: Medium.
HARDINESS: -10 to -15 °C (14 to 5 °F).

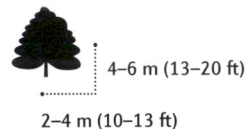

4–6 m (13–20 ft)
2–4 m (10–13 ft)

THUJA PLICATA
Western red cedar
CUPRESSACEAE

This is a conifer that will make a very large evergreen tree when mature, so is only suitable for a garden where it will have that space to grow. In its native forests of western North America, it can grow to heights of over 30 m (100 ft).

For smaller gardens it can also be grown as a fast-growing screening or boundary hedge, for which it is more commonly used.

It is monoecious so has both male and female flowers on the same tree. The male flowers are inconspicuous and the female flowers are also small but are

TREES 137

Thuja plicata

Tilia henryana

borne on the tips of branches. They are reddish-purple. But it is the scale-like leaves that have the fragrance in this conifer and when rubbed they emit a pineapple-like scent.

No pruning should be necessary unless the tree is growing in a hedge, in which case it should be pruned in spring and late summer.
ASPECT: Full sun to partial shade.
FLOWERING: February–April.
SCENTED FOLIAGE: Medium.
HARDINESS: -10 to -15 °C (14 to 5 °F).

8–12 m (26–39 ft)
3–8 m (10–26 ft)

TILIA HENRYANA
Henry's lime
MALVACEAE

Henry's lime is named in honour of the 19th-century Irish plant hunter Augustine Henry, who discovered it in China in 1888. It is still not a tree that is commonly seen growing in domestic gardens, and is somewhat of a rarity, probably in part due to its large size.

Its hanging clusters of fragrant, creamy-white flowers are produced in late summer, and it is one of the last trees to flower, which is great for late-foraging insects.

The tree has wonderful large, oval-shaped leaves that open in spring. They are covered in fine down that gives them a silvery sheen with hints of pink, and their margins have pronounced bristles – like long eyelashes – making them instantly recognisable.

No pruning should be necessary in young trees apart from removing any crossing branches. Any large pruning cuts should be made in summer to reduce the danger of bleeding and allow more rapid healing.
ASPECT: Full sun to partial shade.
FLOWERING: August–September.
SCENT: Medium.
HARDINESS: -10 to -15 °C (14 to 5 °F).

6–10 m (20–33 ft)
5–8 m (16–26 ft)

TILIA TOMENTOSA
Silver lime
MALVACEAE

This is another large lime tree, suited only to the biggest gardens, as it can reach heights of 20 m (70 ft) when fully mature, but is more likely to be 10–12 m (33–40 ft).

This large deciduous tree has erect branching with graceful pendant ends, particularly when in full leaf and flower.

The common name derives from the silvery-white, downy hairs that cover the undersides of the leaves, giving the tree an ever-changing, shimmering appearance when they are moving in a breeze.

Clusters of small, creamy-white or yellow fragrant flowers are borne in profusion during the summer and are highly attractive to foraging bees.

The silver lime also has good autumn colour, with the leaves turning golden-yellow.

No pruning should be necessary in young trees apart from removing any crossing branches. Any large pruning cuts should be made in summer to reduce the danger of bleeding and allow more rapid healing.

ASPECT: Full sun to partial shade.
FLOWERING: June–July.
SCENT: Medium.
HARDINESS: -10 to -15 °C (14 to 5 °F).

6–12 m (20–39 ft)
3–4 m (13–26 ft)

Tilia tomentosa

Glossary

Alternate Arranged at each node on different sides of the stem. Not opposite

Androdioecious Having hermaphrodite and male flowers on separate plants

Anther The pollen-bearing male reproductive organ

Axil The junction of leaf and stem

Axillary Arising in the axil

Basal Located at the base of the plant or stem. Usually leaves

Biennial Germinates and grows in its first year. Flowers and completes its life cycle in its second year

Bract A modified leaf usually at the base of a flower. Sometimes showier than the actual flower

Bulb An underground storage organ made up of swollen leaf bases

Calyx The outer parts of a flower, the sepals

Cambium The layer of cells below the bark of roots and stem that divide to produce new tissue

Climber Also known as lianas, these are plants with long, trailing stems modified to climb by hooks/thorns, suckers and tendrils

Compound leaf A leaf blade that is completely divided, forming leaflets

Coppice Trees or shrubs that are cut back regularly to produce new growth

Corm Resembling a bulb, but replaced with a new corm annually on top of the old one

Corona The cup-shaped floral structure between the tepals and the stamens

Culm A stalk or stem of various grasses and reeds

Cultivar A new plant produced in cultivation rather than in the wild and which has to be propagated vegetatively to remain true

Cuticle Waxy surface of a leaf limiting water loss and protecting against extreme temperatures, high and low

Cyathium A typical inflorescence in the genus *Euphorbia*

Deciduous A plant that sheds its leaves at the end of its growing season, renewing them at the start of the next season

Dioecious Having male and female flowers on separate plants

Endemic Restricted in the wild to a specific geographic region

Epiphyte A plant that does not have roots in the ground, but grows on the surface of other plants

Evergreen A plant that retains most of its leaves throughout the year

Filament A hair-like structure that supports the anther, which together comprise the stamen

Floriferous Plant producing many flowers

Genus A group of species with similar characteristics e.g. *Hamamelis*

Glaucous Bluish-grey in colour

Globular Spherical or rounded in shape

Habitat The place where a plant grows that is often characteristic of a species

Herbaceous A plant that is not woody and dies back to around ground level during the winter period

Hybrid A plant resulting from the cross-fertilisation of two different species

Indumentum A covering of short hairs, often coloured

Inflorescence The flowering part of a plant

Lanceolate Having a narrow outline, usually widest in the middle, tapering towards the tip. Lance-shaped

Lateral At the side

Lax Loose and spreading

Leaflet One of the divisions of a compound leaf

Linear Long thin leaves. Grass-like

Margin Outer edge, usually of a leaf

Monocarpic Flowering once and then dying

Monocot Any flowering plant that has a single embryonic seed leaf. Examples include grasses and palms

Monoecious Male and female flowers on the same plant, but separate

Monotypic A genus with a single species

Native A plant growing in a place where it was not introduced by humans or animals

Node The place on a stem where the leaves are attached

Obovate Oval, but widest above the middle

Panicle A branching stem of stalked flowers

Perennial Any plant living for three years or more. Usually flowering annually, but not always in its first year

Petiole The stalk between the leaf and stem

Photosynthesis The process by which plants use sunlight to convert carbon dioxide into the sugars they use as food

Pinnae A primary division of a pinnate leaf

Pinnate With leaflets arranged on either side of a single stalk

Prostrate Growing flat on the ground, or close to it

Reversion To change back to a previous form or colour

Rhizome A creeping stem that can be above or below the ground

Rosette A cluster of leaves radiating from the same point, usually basal

Semi-evergreen Plants that lose their leaves for a short period of time between the old foliage falling and the new foliage growth

Sepal A segment of the calyx

Sessile Stalkless

Shrub A perennial with woody, much-branched stems

Species Plants with similar characteristics that can interbreed to produce fertile offspring

Simple leaf A leaf that is undivided, where the margins do not reach the midrib

Spine A rigid, sharp structure on a stem or leaf

Stamen The male part of a flower, consisting of both the filament and anther

Stigma The top of the style which receives the pollen

Sub-shrub A small plant with a woody base and herbaceous top

Tendril A thread-like, modified leaflet used to help plants support themselves and climb

Tepal Term used when petals and sepals look alike. Usually in the flowers of bulbous plants, e.g. daffodils

Tree A perennial, usually with a single, woody stem

Trifoliate A compound leaf with three leaflets

Tuber A swollen underground stem or root

Umbel An inflorescence with several flowers all arising from the same point

Undulate Having a wavy margin or surface

Variety Plants that often occur naturally and usually come true from seed. See Cultivar

Whorl The arrangement of flowers or leaves that circle around the same point of the stem

Woody perennial See Shrub

Vegetatively Propagating a plant from parts other than its reproductive parts, e.g. from its roots

Further reading

Brown, George E. Second edition revised and enlarged by Kirkham, Tony (2004)
The Pruning of Trees, Shrubs and Conifers
TIMBER PRESS, LONDON

Fiala, John L. Revised by Vrugtman, Freek (2008)
Lilacs: A Gardener's Encyclopedia
TIMBER PRESS, LONDON

Genders, Roy (1971)
The Scented Wild Flowers of Britain
COLLINS, LONDON

Hall, Tony (2021)
The Kew Gardener's Guide To Growing Roses
FRANCES LINCOLN, LONDON IN ASSOCIATION WITH THE ROYAL BOTANIC GARDENS, KEW

Hillier Nurseries (2019)
The Hillier Manual of Trees & Shrubs
ROYAL HORTICULTURAL SOCIETY, LONDON

Sinclair Rohde, Eleanor (1989)
The Scented Garden
THE MEDICI SOCIETY, LONDON

Verey, Rosemary (1995)
The Scented Garden
MICHAEL JOSEPH, LONDON

Websites

Gardeners' World Magazine: www.gardenersworld.com

Plants For A Future: pfaf.org

Royal Horticultural Society: rhs.org.uk

Trees and Shrubs Online: treesandshrubsonline.org

Plants of the World Online: powo.science.kew.org

Flowering by month

JANUARY

Bulbs
Narcissus papyraceus

Climbers
Clematis cirrhosa

Perennials
Petasites pyrenaicus

Shrubs
Chimonanthus praecox
Daphne bholua
Daphne laureola
Daphne odora 'Aureomarginata'
Hamamelis × intermedia
Lonicera fragrantissima
Lonicera × purpusii 'Winter Beauty'
Sarcococca confusa
Sarcococca hookeriana var. digyna
Viburnum farreri
Viburnum tinus 'Lucidum'

Trees
Azara microphylla
Drimys winteri

FEBRUARY

Bulbs
Galanthus elwesii 'S. Arnott'

Climbers
Clematis cirrhosa
Lonicera japonica

Perennials
Petasites pyrenaicus
Viola odorata

Shrubs
Abeliophyllum distichum
Chimonanthus praecox
Coronilla valentina subsp. glauca
Corylopsis pauciflora
Daphne bholua
Daphne laureola
Daphne odora 'Aureomarginata'
Daphne mezereum
Edgeworthia chrysantha
Erica arborea
Escallonia illinita
Hamamelis × intermedia
Lonicera fragrantissima
Lonicera × purpusii 'Winter Beauty'
Sarcococca confusa
Sarcococca hookeriana var. digyna
Ulex europaeus
Viburnum × bodnantense
Viburnum farreri
Viburnum tinus 'Lucidum'

Trees
Acacia dealbata
Azara microphylla
Citrus × aurantium
Citrus × limon
Drimys winteri
Eucalyptus sp.
Prunus speciosa

Hamamelis 'Jelena'

Chimonthus praecox 'Luteus'

MARCH

Bulbs	Shrubs	
Allium ursinum	*Abeliophyllum distichum*	*Sarcococca confusa*
Galanthus elwesii 'S. Arnott'	*Berberis microphylla*	*Sarcococca hookeriana* var. *digyna*
Hyacinthus orientalis	*Coronilla valentina* subsp. *glauca*	*Ulex europaeus*
Narcissus jonquila	*Corylopsis pauciflora*	*Viburnum* × *bodnantense*
Narcissus poeticus var. *recurvus*	*Daphne bholua*	*Viburnum* × *carlcephalum*
Narcissus tazetta	*Daphne laureola*	*Viburnum carlesii*
Narcissus 'Grand Soleil d'Or'	*Daphne odora* 'Aureomarginata'	*Viburnum farreri*
Tulipa sylvestris	*Daphne mezereum*	*Viburnum tinus* 'Lucidum'
	Edgeworthia chrysantha	
Climbers	*Erica arborea*	**Trees**
Akebia quinata	*Escallonia illinita*	*Acacia dealbata*
Clematis armandii	*Hamamelis* × *intermedia*	*Azara microphylla*
Clematis cirrhosa	*Lonicera fragrantissima*	*Citrus* × *aurantium*
Lonicera japonica	*Lonicera* × *purpusii* 'Winter Beauty'	*Citrus* × *limon*
	Osmanthus delavayi	*Drimys winteri*
Perennials	*Osmanthus* × *burkwoodii*	*Eucalyptus* sp.
Petasites pyrenaicus	*Prunus laurocerasus*	*Magnolia doltsopa*
Primula vulgaris	*Rhododendron* 'Loderi King George'	*Magnolia stellata*
Viola odorata	*Ribes odoratum*	*Prunus speciosa*

Choisya × *dewitteana*

Rhododendron 'Loderi King George'

Viburnum carlesii

FLOWERING BY MONTH 143

APRIL

Annuals and Biennials
Erysimum cheiri
Matthiola longipetala

Bulbs
Allium ursinum
Convallaria majalis
Freesia refracta
Fritillaria imperialis
Hyacinthoides non-scripta
Hyacinthus orientalis
Narcissus jonquilla
Narcissus poeticus var. *recurvus*
Narcissus tazetta
Narcissus 'Grand Soleil d'Or'
Polygonatum odoratum
Tulipa sylvestris
Tulipa hybrids

Climbers
Akebia quinata
Clematis armandii
Clematis montana
Lonicera japonica
Stauntonia coriacea
Stauntonia latifolia

Herbs
Salvia rosmarinus

Perennials
Disporopsis pernyi
Galium odoratum
Primula veris
Primula vulgaris
Viola odorata

Shrubs
Berberis microphylla
Coronilla valentina subsp. *glauca*
Cytisus 'Porlock'
Dipelta floribunda
Edgeworthia chrysantha
Elaeagnus umbellata
Erica arborea
Escallonia illinita
Osmanthus delavayi
Osmanthus × *burkwoodii*
Prunus laurocerasus
Rhododendron 'Loderi King George'
Ribes odoratum
Skimmia × *confusa* 'Kew Green'
Skimmia japonica 'Fragrant Cloud'
Syringa laciniata
Syringa meyeri
Syringa vulgaris cultivar
Syringa × *hyacinthiflora* cultivars
Ulex europaeus
Viburnum × *bodnantense*
Viburnum × *carlcephalum*
Viburnum carlesii

Trees
Acacia dealbata
Citrus ×*aurantium*
Citrus ×*limon*
Citrus limetta
Crataegus monogyna
Drimys winteri
Eucalyptus sp.
Magnolia doltsopa
Magnolia figo
Magnolia stellata
Prunus serrulata 'Jo-Nioi'
Prunus serrulata 'Taki-Nioi'
Prunus 'Shizuka'
Prunus speciosa

Syringa vulgaris 'Le Notra'

Prunus 'Taki-Nioi'

MAY

Annuals and Biennials
Cota austriaca
Erysimum cheiri
Matthiola longipetala
Nicotiana alata

Bulbs
Allium ursinum
Convallaria majalis
Freesia refracta
Fritillaria imperialis
Hemerocallis lilioasphodelus
Hyacinthoides non-scripta
Narcissus poeticus var. *recurvus*
Narcissus tazetta
Polygonatum odoratum
Tulipa hybrids

Climbers
Akebia quinata
Clematis armandii
Clematis montana
Stauntonia coriacea
Stauntonia latifolia
Wisteria floribunda
Wisteria sinensis

Herbs
Allium schoenoprasum
Laurus nobilis
Salvia rosmarinus
Thymus vulgaris

Perennials
Galium odoratum
Geranium macrorrhizum
Hesperis matronalis
Lunaria rediviva
Myrrhis odorata
Phlox divaricata
Primula veris
Primula vulgaris

Shrubs
Azara serrata
Buddleja alternifolia
Buddleja globosa
Chionanthus virginicus
Choisya ternata
Cytisus 'Porlock'
Dipelta floribunda
Elaeagnus umbellata
Itea virginica
Prunus lusitanica
Rhododendron luteum
Rosa roxburghii
Sambucus nigra
Skimmia × *confusa* 'Kew Green'
Skimmia japonica 'Fragrant Cloud'
Syringa laciniata
Syringa meyeri
Syringa tomentella subsp. *yunnanensis*
Syringa vulgaris cultivars
Syringa × *hyacinthiflora* cultivars
Ulex europaeus
Viburnum × *bodnantense*
Viburnum × *carlcephalum*
Viburnum carlesii

Trees
Citrus × *aurantium*
Citrus × *limon*
Crataegus monogyna
Ehretia dicksonii
Eucalyptus sp.
Magnolia doltsopa
Magnolia figo
Magnolia sieboldii
Magnolia stellata
Paulownia tomentosa
Prunus serrulata 'Jo-Nioi'
Prunus serrulata 'Taki-Nioi'
Prunus 'Shizuka'

Convallaria majalis

Prunus lusitanica

Buddleja globosa

JUNE

Annuals and Biennials
Borago officinalis
Cota austriaca
Erysimum cheiri
Heliotropium arborescens
Ipomoea alba
Lathyrus odoratus
Lobularia maritima
Matthiola longipetala
Mirabilis jalapa
Nicotiana alata
Oenothera biennis
Reseda odorata

Bulbs
Cardiocrinum giganteum
Chlidanthus fragrans
Hemerocallis lilioasphodelus
Lilium martagon
Lilium regale
Polygonatum odoratum

Climbers
Clematis montana
Jasminum officinale
Rosa 'Compassion'
Rosa helenae
Rosa 'Kew Rambler'
Rosa 'Paul's Himalayan Musk'
Rosa 'Rambling Rector'
Rosa 'Shropshire Lass'
Rosa 'Generous Gardener'
Trachelospermum asiaticum
Trachelospermum jasminoides
Wisteria floribunda
Wisteria sinensis

Herbs
Allium schoenoprasum
Angelica archangelica
Anthriscus cerefolium
Borago officinalis
Helichrysum italicum
Laurus nobilis
Levisticum officinale
Matricaria chamomilla
Melissa officinalis
Mentha × *piperita*
Monarda didyma
Ocimum basilicum
Salvia rosmarinus
Salvia vulgaris
Tanacetum parthenium
Tanacetum vulgare
Thymus × *citriodorus*
Thymus vulgaris

Perennials
Achillea millefolium
Aquilegia fragrans
Cosmos atrosanguineus
Dianthus barbatus
Dianthus caryophyllus
Disporopsis pernyi
Galium odoratum
Geranium macrorrhizum

Cardiocrinum giganteum

Santolina chamaecyparissus

Hesperis matronalis	*Cytisus* 'Porlock'	*Santolina chamaecyparissus*
Lunaria rediviva	*Dipelta floribunda*	*Spartium junceum*
Matthiola incana	*Itea virginica*	*Syringa meyeri*
Myrrhis odorata	*Lavandula angustifolia*	*Syringa tomentella* subsp. *yunnanensis*
Nepeta cataria	*Lavandula* × *intermedia*	*Syringa vulgaris* cultivars
Paeonia lactiflora	*Lavandula stoechas*	*Zabelia triflora*
Phlox divaricata	*Ligustrum vulgare*	*Zenobia pulverulenta*
Phlox paniculata	*Philadelphus coronarius*	
Zaluzianskya ovata	*Philadelphus* 'Belle Etoile'	**Trees**
	Philadelphus microphyllus	*Albizia julibrissin*
Shrubs	*Philadelphus* 'Lemoinei'	*Citrus* × *aurantium*
Abelia × *grandiflora*	*Philadelphus* 'Virginal'	*Citrus* × *limon*
Argyrocytisus battandieri	*Prunus lusitanica*	*Ehretia dicksonii*
Azara serrata	*Rhododendron luteum*	*Eucalyptus* sp.
Buddleja alternifolia	*Rosa* × *alba* 'Alba Semiplena'	*Magnolia figo*
Buddleja globosa	*Rosa* × *centifolia*	*Magnolia sieboldii*
Buddleja salviifolia	*Rosa* 'Charles Darwin'	*Magnolia stellata*
Calycanthus floridus	*Rosa* 'Felicia'	*Paulownia tomentosa*
Chionanthus virginicus	*Rosa* 'Roseraie de l'Haÿ'	*Ptelea trifoliata*
Choisya ternata	*Rosa roxburghii*	*Tilia tomentosa*
Cistus creticus	*Rosa rugosa*	
Cistus ladanifer	*Sambucus nigra*	

Trachelospermum jasminoides

JULY

Annuals and Biennials
Borago officinalis
Cota austriaca
Dianthus barbatus
Dianthus caryophyllus
Heliotropium arborescens
Ipomoea alba
Lathyrus odoratus
Lobularia maritima
Matthiola longipetala
Mirabilis jalapa
Nicotiana alata
Oenothera biennis
Reseda odorata

Bulbs
Cardiocrinum giganteum
Chlidanthus fragrans
Lilium candidum
Lilium martagon
Lilium regale
Ornithogalum candicans

Climbers
Clematis flammula
Clematis rehderiana
Cochliasanthus caracalla
Jasminum officinale
Lonicera periclymenum
Rosa 'Compassion'
Rosa helenae
Rosa 'Kew Rambler'
Rosa 'Paul's Himalayan Musk'
Rosa 'Rambling Rector'
Rosa 'Shropshire Lass'
Rosa 'Generous Gardener'
Trachelospermum asiaticum
Trachelospermum jasminoides

Herbs
Allium schoenoprasum
Aloysia citrodora
Anethum graveolens
Angelica archangelica
Anthriscus cerefolium
Artemisia dracunculus
Borago officinalis
Foeniculum vulgare
Helichrysum italicum
Humulus lupulus
Hyssopus officinalis
Levisticum officinale
Matricaria chamomilla
Melissa officinalis
Mentha × *piperita*
Monarda didyma
Ocimum basilicum
Origanum vulgare
Salvia rosmarinus
Salvia vulgaris
Tanacetum parthenium
Tanacetum vulgare
Thymus × *citriodorus*
Thymus vulgaris

Myrtus communis

Magnolia virginiana

Lilium regale

Perennials	*Buddleja* 'Black Knight'	*Rosa* × *alba* 'Alba Semiplena'
Achillea millefolium	*Buddleja globosa*	*Rosa* × *centifolia*
Aquilegia fragrans	*Buddleja salviifolia*	*Rosa* 'Charles Darwin'
Artemisia absinthium	*Buddleja* × *weyeriana* 'Sungold'	*Rosa* 'Felicia'
Clinopodium nepeta	*Calycanthus floridus*	*Rosa* 'Roseraie de l'Haÿ'
Cosmos atrosanguineus	*Cistus creticus*	*Rosa rugosa*
Dianthus barbatus	*Cistus ladanifer*	*Sambucus nigra*
Dianthus caryophyllus	*Clerodendrum trichotomum*	*Santolina chamaecyparissus*
Disporopsis pernyi	*Clethra alnifolia*	*Spartium junceum*
Galium odoratum	*Clethra barbinervis*	*Syringa tomentella* subsp. *yunnanensis*
Geranium macrorrhizum	*Colletia hystrix*	*Zabelia triflora*
Hesperis matronalis	*Hoheria glabrata*	*Zenobia pulverulenta*
Lunaria rediviva	*Itea ilicifolia*	
Matthiola incana	*Itea virginica*	**Trees**
Myrrhis odorata	*Lavandula angustifolia*	*Albizia julibrissin*
Nepeta cataria	*Lavandula* × *intermedia*	*Catalpa ovata*
Paeonia lactiflora	*Lavandula stoechas*	*Citrus* × *aurantium*
Phlox paniculata	*Ligustrum vulgare*	*Citrus* × *limon*
Zaluzianskya ovata	*Myrtus communis*	*Eucalyptus* sp.
	Philadelphus coronarius	*Magnolia sieboldii*
Shrubs	*Philadelphus* 'Belle Etoile'	*Magnolia stellata*
Abelia × *grandiflora*	*Philadelphus microphyllus*	*Ptelea trifoliata*
Argyrocytisus battandieri	*Philadelphus* 'Lemoinei'	*Tilia tomentosa*
Buddleja alternifolia	*Philadelphus* 'Virginal'	

Rosa 'Generous Gardner'

Rosa × *centifolia*

FLOWERING BY MONTH

AUGUST

Annuals and Biennials
Borago officinalis
Cota austriaca
Dianthus barbatus
Dianthus caryophyllus
Heliotropium arborescens
Ipomoea alba
Lathyrus odoratus
Lobularia maritima
Mirabilis jalapa
Nicotiana alata
Oenothera biennis
Reseda odorata

Bulbs
Gladiolus murielae
Lilium candidum
Lilium martagon
Ornithogalum candicans

Climbers
Clematis flammula
Clematis rehderiana
Cochliasanthus caracalla
Jasminum officinale
Lonicera periclymenum
Rosa 'Compassion'
Rosa 'Shropshire Lass'
Rosa 'Generous Gardener'
Trachelospermum asiaticum
Trachelospermum jasminioides

Herbs
Aloysia citrodora
Anethum graveolens
Anthriscus cerefolium
Artemisia dracunculus
Borago officinalis
Foeniculum vulgare
Helichrysum italicum
Humulus lupulus
Hyssopus officinalis
Levisticum officinale
Matricaria chamomilla
Melissa officinalis
Mentha × *piperita*
Monarda didyma
Ocimum basilicum
Origanum vulgare
Salvia rosmarinus
Salvia vulgaris
Tanacetum parthenium
Tanacetum vulgare
Thymus × *citriodorus*

Perennials
Achillea millefolium
Artemisia absinthium
Clinopodium nepeta
Cosmos atrosanguineus
Dianthus barbatus
Dianthus caryophyllus
Geranium macrorrhizum
Lunaria rediviva
Matthiola incana
Nepeta cataria
Phlox paniculata
Zaluzianskya ovata

Shrubs
Abelia × *grandiflora*
Buddleja 'Black Knight'
Buddleja × *weyeriana* 'Sungold'
Cistus creticus
Cistus ladanifer
Clerodendrum bungei
Clerodendrum trichotomum
Clethra alnifolia
Clethra barbinervis
Colletia hystrix
Hoheria glabrata
Itea ilicifolia
Lavandula angustifolia
Lavandula × *intermedia*
Lavandula stoechas
Ligustrum vulgare
Myrtus communis
Rosa 'Charles Darwin'
Rosa 'Felicia'
Rosa 'Roseraie de l'Haÿ'
Rosa rugosa
Santolina chamaecyparissus
Spartium junceum
Vitex agnus-castus

Trees
Albizia julibrissin
Catalpa ovata
Citrus × *aurantium*
Citrus × *limon*
Citrus limetta
Heptacodium miconioides
Magnolia grandiflora
Tilia henryana

Clematis flammula

Clethra alnifolia

Lavandula

FLOWERING BY MONTH 151

SEPTEMBER

Annuals and Biennials	Herbs	Shrubs
Borago officinalis	*Anethum graveolens*	*Abelia* × *grandiflora*
Dianthus barbatus	*Anthriscus cerefolium*	*Buddleja* 'Black Knight'
Dianthus caryophyllus	*Borago officinalis*	*Buddleja* × *weyeriana* 'Sungold'
Heliotropium arborescens	*Helichrysum italicum*	*Clerodendrum bungei*
Ipomoea alba	*Humulus lupulus*	*Clerodendrum trichotomum*
Lathyrus odoratus	*Hyssopus officinalis*	*Colletia hystrix*
Lobularia maritima	*Origanum vulgare*	*Lavandula angustifolia*
Nicotiana alata	*Salvia rosmarinus*	*Lavandula* × *intermedia*
Oenothera biennis	*Tanacetum parthenium*	*Lavandula stoechas*
Reseda odorata		*Rosa* 'Charles Darwin'
	Perennials	*Rosa* 'Felicia'
Bulbs	*Achillea millefolium*	*Rosa* 'Roseraie de l'Haÿ'
Gladiolus murielae	*Clinopodium nepeta*	*Spartium junceum*
Ornithogalum candicans	*Cosmos atrosanguineus*	*Vitex agnus-castus*
	Dianthus barbatus	
Climbers	*Dianthus caryophyllus*	**Trees**
Clematis flammula	*Geranium macrorrhizum*	*Citrus* × *aurantium*
Clematis rehderiana	*Nepeta cataria*	*Citrus* × *limon*
Cochliasanthus caracalla	*Phlox paniculata*	*Heptacodium miconioides*
Lonicera periclymenum	*Zaluzianskya ovata*	*Magnolia grandiflora*
Rosa 'Compassion'		*Tilia henryana*
Rosa 'Generous Gardener'		

Clerodendrum trichotomum

Mandevilla laxa

152 GARDENING WITH SCENTED PLANTS

Tilia henryi

FLOWERING BY MONTH 153

OCTOBER

Annuals and Biennials
Heliotropium arborescens
Nicotiana alata
Reseda odorata

Bulbs
Gladiolus murielae

Climbers
Clematis rehderiana
Rosa 'Compassion'

Herbs
Anethum graveolens
Anthriscus cerefolium
Borago officinalis
Salvia rosmarinus

Shrubs
Abelia × *grandiflora*
Clerodendrum bungei
Colletia hystrix
Elaeagnus × *submacrophylla*
Sarcococca hookeriana var. *digyna*
Vitex agnus-castus

NOVEMBER

Climbers
Clematis cirrhosa

Herbs
Borago officinalis
Salvia rosmarinus

Shrubs
Elaeagnus × *submacrophylla*
Sarcococca hookeriana var. *digyna*
Viburnum farreri

Albizia julbrissin

Viburnum farreri

DECEMBER

Bulbs
Narcissus papyraceus

Climbers
Clematis cirrhosa

Herbs
Salvia rosmarinus

Perennials
Petasites pyrenaicus

Shrubs
Chimonanthus praecox
Hamamelis × intermedia
Lonicera fragrantissima
Lonicera × purpusii 'Winter Beauty'
Sarcococca confusa
Sarcococca hookeriana var. *digyna*
Viburnum farreri
Viburnum tinus 'Lucidum'

Chimonanthus praecox

Osmanthus × burkwoodii

Lonicera fragrantissima

FLOWERING BY MONTH 155

Flower colours

RED

Calycanthus floridus
Daphne mezereum
Dianthus barbatus
Dianthus caryophyllus
Edgeworthia chrysantha 'Red Dragon'
Erysimum cheiri
Monarda didyma
Matthiola incana
Phlox paniculata
Syringa vulgaris cultivars
Syringa × *hyacinthiflora* cultivars
Tulipa hybrids

Edgeworthia 'Red Dragon'

Erysimum 'Winter Passion'

Lavandula viridis

156   GARDENING WITH SCENTED PLANTS

GREEN/GREENISH

Angelica archangelica
Daphne laureola
Itea ilicifolia
Levisticum officinale
Matthiola incana
Polygonatum odoratum
Ptelea trifoliata
Stauntonia latifolia
Tulipa hybrids

BLUE

Borago officinalis
Heliotropium arborescens
Hyacinthoides non-scripta
Hyssopus officinalis
Phlox divaricata
Viola odorata
Wisteria floribunda

Daphne laureola

Hyacinthoides non-scripta

Borago officinalis

FLOWER COLOURS 157

PURPLE/MAUVE	
Allium schoenoprasum	*Nicotiana alata*
Buddleja 'Black Knight'	*Origanum vulgare*
Dianthus barbatus	*Phlox paniculata*
Dianthus caryophyllus	*Rosa* 'Roseraie de l'Haÿ'
Lathyrus odoratus	*Salvia rosmarinus*
Lavandula angustifolia	*Salvia vulgaris*
Lavandula × *intermedia*	*Syringa vulgaris* cultivars
Lavandula stoechas	*Syringa* × *hyacinthiflora* cultivars
Lilium martagon	*Tanacetum parthenium*
Mentha × *piperita*	*Thymus* × *citriodorus*
Mirabilis jalapa	*Tulipa* hybrids
Nepeta cataria	*Wisteria sinensis*

ORANGE
Berberis microphylla
Buddleja globosa
Erysimum 'Rysi Copper'
Fritillaria imperialis
Narcissus tazetta
Tulipa hybrids

Tulbaghia violacea

Erysimum 'Rysi Copper'

Buddleja 'Black Knight'

Berberis microphylla

LILAC

Buddleja alternifolia
Buddleja salviifolia
Clinopodium nepeta
Dianthus barbatus
Dianthus caryophyllus
Lavandula stoechas
Matthiola longipetala
Nicotiana alata
Petasites pyrenaicus
Syringa laciniata
Syringa meyeri
Tulipa hybrids
Vitex agnus-castus
Wisteria sinensis

Buddleja alternifolia

Syringa laciniata

Lathryus 'Chrissie'

FLOWER COLOURS   159

PINK

Cistus creticus
Clerodendrum bungei
Daphne bholua
Daphne odora 'Aureomarginata'
Dianthus barbatus
Dianthus caryophyllus
Dipelta floribunda
Geranium macrorrhizum
Lavandula stoechas
Matthiola incana
Mirabilis jalapa
Nicotiana alata
Origanum vulgare
Paeonia lactiflora
Phlox paniculata
Rosa × *centifolia*
Rosa 'Felicia'
Rosa 'Generous Gardener'
Rosa 'Kew Rambler'
Rosa 'Paul's Himalayan Musk'
Rosa roxburghii
Rosa rugosa
Rosa 'Shropshire Lass'
Tulipa hybrids
Thymus vulgaris
Viburnum × *bodnantense*

Clematis 'Apple Blossom'

Rosa 'Kew Rambler'

CREAM

Cardiocrinum giganteum
Catalpa ovata
Chimonanthus praecox
Clematis cirrhosa
Clematis rehderiana
Cochliasanthus caracalla
Elaeagnus × *submacrophylla*
Elaeagnus umbellata
Freesia refracta
Lonicera periclymenum
Magnolia virginiana
Matthiola incana
Matthiola longipetala
Stauntonia coriacea
Tilia henryana
Tilia tomentosa
Trachelospermum asiaticum
Tulipa hybrids

Jasminum officinale 'Devon Cream'

Eleagnus umbellata

YELLOW

Acacia dealbata	*Cytisus 'Porlock'*	*Primula veris*
Anethum graveolens	*Edgeworthia chrysantha*	*Primula vulgaris*
Aquilegia fragrans	*Foeniculum vulgare*	*Reseda odorata*
Argyrocytisus battandieri	*Hamamelis × intermedia*	*Rhododendron luteum*
Artemisia absinthium	*Helichrysum italicum*	*Ribes odoratum*
Artemisia dracunculus	*Hemerocallis lilioasphodelus*	*Rosa 'Charles Darwin'*
Azara microphylla	*Lathyrus odoratus*	*Santolina chamaecyparissus*
Azara serrata	*Lonicera japonica*	*Spartium junceum*
Chimonanthus praecox	*Magnolia figo*	*Tanacetum vulgare*
Chlidanthus fragrans	*Narcissus jonquila*	*Tulipa sylvestris*
Coronilla valentina subsp. *glauca*	*Nicotiana alata*	*Tulipa* hybrids
Corylopsis pauciflora	*Oenothera biennis*	*Ulex europaeus*

Argyrocytisus battandieri

Mirabilis jalapa

Santolina chamaecyparissus

WHITE

Abelia × *grandiflora*	*Gladiolus murielae*	*Prunus laurocerasus*
Abeliophyllum distichum	*Hoheria glabrata*	*Prunus lusitanica*
Achillea millefolium	*Ipomoea alba*	*Rhododendron* 'Loderi King George'
Allium ursinum	*Jasminum officinale*	*Rosa helenae*
Aloysia citrodora	*Lilium candidum*	*Rosa* 'Rambling Rector'
Anthriscus cerefolium	*Lilium regale*	*Rosa* × *alba* 'Alba Semiplena'
Borago officinalis	*Lonicera fragrantissima*	*Sarcococca confusa*
Choisya ternata	*Lonicera* × *purpusii* 'Winter Beauty'	*Sarcococca hookeriana* var. *digyna*
Clematis armandii	*Matthiola incana*	*Skimmia japonica* 'Fragrant Cloud'
Clematis flammula	*Matricaria chamomilla*	*Skimmia* × *confusa* 'Kew Green'
Clerodendrum trichotomum	*Melissa officinalis*	*Syringa tomentella* subsp. *yunnanensis*
Clethra alnifolia	*Mirabilis jalapa*	*Tanacetum parthenium*
Clethra barbinervis	*Narcissus papyraceus*	*Trachelospermum jasminoides*
Colletia hystrix	*Narcissus poeticus* var. *recurvus*	*Tulipa* hybrids
Dianthus barbatus	*Nicotiana alata*	*Viburnum farreri*
Dianthus caryophyllus	*Ornithogalum candicans*	*Viburnum tinus* 'Lucidum'
Erica arborea	*Philadelphus coronarius*	*Viburnum* × *carlcephalum*
Erysimum cheiri	*Philadelphus* 'Belle Etoile'	*Zabelia triflora*
Escallonia illinita	*Philadelphus microphyllus*	*Zaluzianskya ovata*
Galanthus elwesii 'S. Arnott'	*Philadelphus* 'Lemoinei'	*Zenobia pulverulenta*
Galium odoratum	*Philadelphus* 'Virginal'	

Prunus serrulata 'Jo-Nioi'

Syringa vulgaris 'Monument'

164 GARDENING WITH SCENTED PLANTS

Achillea millefolium

Plants with scented foliage

ANNUALS
Cota austriaca

BULBS
Allium ursinum
Allium schoenoprasum

HERBS
Aloysia citrodora
Anethum graveolens
Anthriscus cerefolium
Artemisia dranunculus
Borago officinalis
Foeniculum vulgare
Helichrysum italicum
Hyssopus officinalis
Laurus nobilis
Levisticum officinale
Matricaria chamomilla
Melissa officinalis
Mentha × piperita
Monarda didyma
Ocimum basilicum
Origanum vulgare
Salvia rosmarinus
Salvia vulgaris
Tanacetum parthenium
Tanacetum vulgare
Thymus × citriodorus
Thymus vulgaris

PERENNIALS
Achillea millefolium
Artemisia absinthium
Clinopodium nepeta
Galium odoratum
Geranium macrorrhizum
Myrrhis odorata
Nepeta cataria

SHRUBS
Calycanthus floridus
Choisya ternata
Cistus creticus
Cistus ladanifer
Clerodendrum bungei
Escallonia illinita
Ficus carica
Lavandula angustifolia
Lavandula × intermedia
Lavandula stoechas
Myrtus communis
Santolina chamaecyparissus
Vitex agnus-castus

TREES
Calocedrus decurrens
Cercidiphyllum japonicum
Eucalyptus sp.
Heptacodium miconioides
Ptelea trifoliata

Aloysia citrodora

Purple sage

Foeniculum vulgare

Plants for wildlife

ANNUALS/BIENNIALS
Cota austriaca
Heliotropium arborescens
Lobularia maritima
Oenothera biennis

BULBS
Allium ursinum
Convallaria majalis
Crocus chrysanthus
Galanthus elwesii 'S. Arnott'
Hyacinthoides non-scripta
Narcissus jonquilla
Narcissus poeticus
Narcissus tazetta
Polygonatum odoratum

CLIMBERS
Clematis armandii
Clematis cirrhosa
Clematis flammula
Clematis montana
Lonicera japonica
Lonicera periclymenum
Stauntonia latifolia
Stauntonia coriacea
Wisteria sinensis

HERBS
Allium schoenoprasum
Artemisia dracunculus
Borago officinalis
Hyssopus officinalis
Laurus nobilis
Matricaria chamomilla
Mentha × piperita
Ocimum basilicum

Origanum vulgare
Salvia officinalis
Salvia vulgaris
Tanecetum vulgare
Thymus × citriodorus
Thymus vulgaris

PERENNIALS
Achillea millefolium
Aquilegia fragrans
Clinopodium nepeta
Disporopsis pernyi
Geranium macrorrhizum
Hesperis matronalis
Lunaria rediviva
Matthiola incana
Myrrhis odorata
Nepeta cataria
Petasites pyrenaicus
Primula veris
Primula vulgaris
Tanacetum vulgare
Viola odorata

SHRUBS
Abelia × grandiflora
Abeliophyllum distichum
Berberis microphylla
Buddleja spp.
Cistus ladanifer
Clethra alnifolia
Colletia hystrix
Coronilla valentina subsp. glauca
Corylopsis pauciflora
Daphne bholua
Daphne laureola
Eleaegnus × submacrophylla

Elaeagnus umbellata
Erica arborea
Hamamelis × intermedia
Lavandula spp.
Ligustrum vulgare
Lonicera fragrantissima
Myrtus communis
Osmanthus delavayi
Osmanthus × burkwoodii
Philadelphus spp.
Prunus laurocerasus
Rosa roxburghii
Sarcococca confusa
Sarcococca hookeriana var. digyna
Syringa vulgaris
Ulex europaeus
Viburnum × bodnantense
Viburnum × carlcephalum
Viburnum carlesii
Viburnum farreri

TREES
Catalpa ovata
Citrus spp.
Cordyline australis
Crataegus monogyna
Ligustrum lucidum
Paulownia tomentosa
Prunus serrulata 'Jo-Nioi'
Prunus serrulata 'Taki-Nioi'
Prunus 'Shizuka'
Prunus speciosa
Ptelea trifoliata
Tilia henryana
Tilia tomentosa

OVERLEAF
Hesperis matronalis

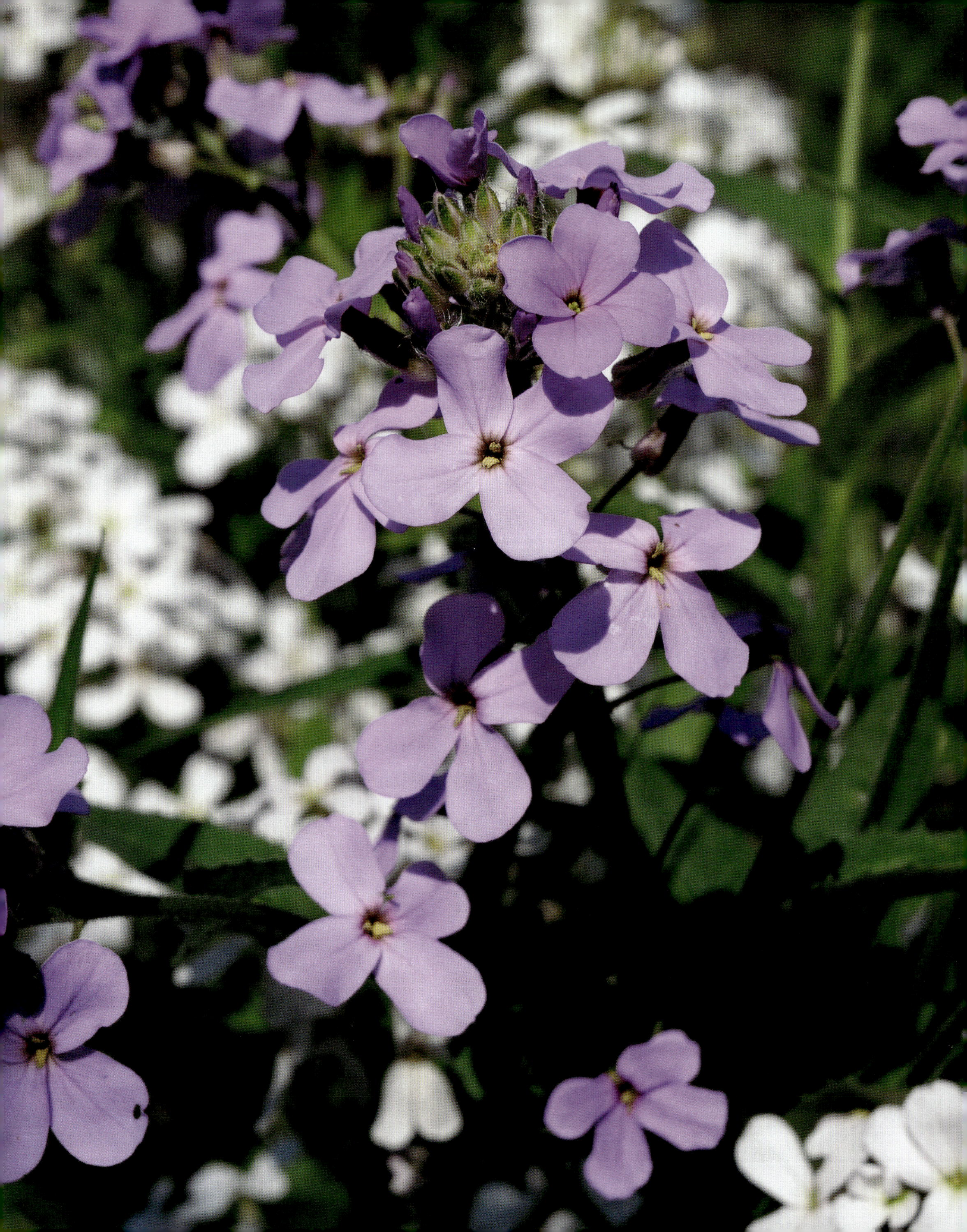

Index

Entries with a photograph are indicated by a **bold** page number.

A
Abelia
   chinensis 82
   uniflora 82
   × *grandiflora* **82**, 147, 149, 150, 152, 154, 164, 167
Abeliophyllum distichum 82, **83**, 142, 143, 164, 167
Abyssinian gladiolus 32
Acacia dealbata **124**, 142, 143, 144, 162
Achillea
   'Cerise Queen' 70
   'Lilac Beauty' 70
   millefolium **70**, 146, 149, 150, 152, **164**, 166, 167
   'Terracotta' 70
Adam's needle **121**
Akebia quinata **42**, 143, 144, 145
Albizia julibrissin **124**, 147, 149, 150, **154**
   'Summer Chocolate' 124
alder 14
Allium
   schoenoprasum **56**, 145, 146, 148, 158, 158, 166, 167
   ursinum **28**, 143, 144, 145, 164, 166, 167
Aloysia citrodora **56**, 148, 150, 164, **166**
Amaryllidaceae 28, 29, 30, 35, 36, 38, 56
Anethum graveolens 57, **58**, 148, 150, 152, 154, 162, 166
angelica 57
Angelica archangelica **57**, 146, 148, 157
annual honesty 74, 75
Anthemis austriaca 20
Anthriscus cerefolium **57**, 146, 148, 150, 152, 154, 164, 166
Apiaceae 57, 59, 61, 75
Apocynaceae 47, 51
Aquilegia fragrans **70**, 146, 149, 162, 167
Argyrocytisus battandieri **83**, 147, 149, **162**
Armand clematis 42
Artemisia
   absinthium **70**, 149, 150, 162, 166
   dracunculus **58**, 148, 150, 162, 166, 167
Asiatic jasmine 51
Asparagaceae 29, 33, 37, 38, 72, 121, 126

Asphodelaceae 32
Asteraceae 20, 58, 59, 62, 65, 70, 71, 77, 111
autumn olive **97**
azalea 106
   swamp 106
   western 106
   yellow 106
Azalea pontica 106
azara
   box leaf **83**, 84
   saw-toothed **84**
Azara
   microphylla 10, **83**, 142, 143, 162
   serrata **84**, 145, 147, 162
   'Variegata' **83**, **84**

B
banana magnolia 132
basil 63
   cinnamon 63
   lemon 63
   lime 63
   sweet 63
bay tree 61
Berberidaceae 84
Berberis microphylla **84**, 143, 144, **158**, 167
bergamot 63
Bignoniaceae 125
big-root cranesbill **74**
blue wattle **124**
bluebell 14
   common **33**
   Spanish 33
bodnant viburnum **118**
borage **58**
   white-flowered **12**
Boraginaceae 21, 58, 129
Borago officinalis **58**, 146, **147**, 157, 164
   'Alba' **58**, 148, 150, 152, 154, 166, 167
   'Bill Archer' 58
box
   Christmas box **111**
   common 83
   sweet **111**
box leaf azara **83**, 84

box-leaved barberry **84**
Brassicaceae 20, 24, 74, 75
bristly colletia **92**
broad-leaved sausage vine **50**
Brompton stocks 75
broom 93
   Moroccan **83**
   pineapple **83**
   Spanish **112**
Buddleja
   alternifolia **85**, 145, 147, 149, **159**
   davidii 86, 87
      'Black Knight' **85**, 149, 150, 152, **158**
   globosa **86**, 87, **145**, 147, 149, 158
   'Golden Glow' 86
   salviifolia 86, 147, 149, **159**
   'Sungold' 86
   × *weyeriana* 'Sungold' **86**, 149, 150, 152
buffalo currant **107**
bunch-flowered narcissus **36**
Burkwood osmanthus **103**
burr rose **110**
butterfly bush **15**, **85**
   fountain **85**
   'Sungold' 86
Buxaceae 111
Buxus sempervirens 83

C
cabbage rose **108**
cabbage tree **126**
Calamintha nepeta **71**
Calocedrus decurrens 124, **125**, 166
Calycanthaceae 87
Calycanthus floridus **87**, 147, 149, 156, 166
camomile 13
Cannabaceae 60
Caprifoliaceae 46, 47, 82, 96, 99, 102, 120
Cardiocrinum giganteum **28**, **146**, 148, 161
carnation 72
Carolina allspice **87**
Caryophyllaceae 20, 72
Castanea sativa **110**
Catalpa ovata **125**, 149, 150, 161, 167
catmint **76**

INDEX   169

lesser 76
cedar
 incense 124
 western red 137, **138**
Cercidiphyllaceae 125
Cercidiphyllum japonicum 8, **125**, 166
chaste tree 120
cherry 14
 'Jo-Nioi' **134**
 Oshima 136, **137**
 Shizuka **135**, 136
 'Taki-Nioi' **136**
cherry laurel 105
cherry pie plant 21
chestnut rose 110
Chilean jasmine 47
Chimonanthus praecox 9, **87**, 142, **155**, 161, 162
 'Grandiflorus' 87
 'Luteus' **87**, 142
Chinese fringe tree 126
Chinese magnolia 132
Chinese peony 76
Chinese wisteria 53
Chinese witch hazel 99
Chionanthus
 retusus **126**
 virginicus **88**, 145, 147
chives **56**, 57
Chlidanthus fragrans **29**, 146, 148, 162
chocolate cosmos 71
chocolate vine 42
Choisya
 'Sundance' 88, **89**
 ternata 88, **89**, 145, 147, 164, 166
 × *dewitteana* 'Aztec Pearl' 88, **89**, **143**
Christmas box 111
cinnamon basil 63
Cistaceae 89
Cistus
 creticus 90, 147, 149, 150, 160, 166
 ladanifer 89, **90**, 147, 149, 150, 166, 167
Citrus **127**, 167
 reticulata 127
 × *aurantium* 142, 143, 144, 145, 147, 149, 150, 152
 f. *aurantium* 127
 × *limon* 127, 142, 143, 144, 145, 147, 149, 150, 152
 × *sinensis* 127
clematis
 Armand 42

evergreen 43
Himalayan 44
sweet autumn 44
Clematis
 armandii 42, 143, 144, 145, 164, 167
 'Apple Blossom' 42, 43, **160**
 cirrhosa 43, 142, 143, 154, 155, 161, 167
 'Freckles' 43
 'Jingle Bells' 43
 flammula 43, 148, 150, 152, **151**, 164, 167
 montana 44, 144, 145, 146, 167
 'Freda' 44
 'Grandiflora' 44
 'Pink Perfection' 44
 'Rubens' 44
 'Warwickshire Rose' 44
 rehderiana 44, 148, 150, 152, 154, 161
 'Rubromarginata' 45
 ternifolia 44
 × *triternata* 45
Clerodendrum
 bungei 90, 150, 152, 154, 160, 166
 trichotomum 91, 149, 150, **152**, 164
Clethra
 alnifolia 91, 149, 150, **151**, 164, 167
 'Ruby Spice' 91
 barbinervis **91**, 149, 150, 164
Clethraceae 91
Clinopodium nepeta 71, 76, 149, 150, 152, 159, 166, 167
 'White Cloud' 71
Cochliasanthus caracalla 45, 148, 150, 152, 161
Colletia hystrix **92**, 149, 150, 152, 154, 164, 167
 'Rosea' 92
common bluebell 33
common box 83
common elder 107
common gorse 117
common hawthorn 128
common honeysuckle 47
common hyacinth 33
common jasmine 46
common lavender 101
common lilac **114**, 116
common mock orange 104
common myrtle 102, **103**
common privet **102**
common sage 65
common thyme 66, **67**
Convallaria majalis **29**, 144, **145**, 167

var. *rosea* 29
Convolvulaceae 21
Cordyline australis **126**, 167
corkscrew flower 45
corn camomile 20
corn marigolds 20
corncockle 20
Cornish palm 126
Coronilla
 'Citrina' 92, **93**
 glauca 92
 valentina subsp. *glauca* 92, 142, 143, 144, 162, 167
Corylopsis pauciflora **93**, 142, 143, 162, 167
Cosmos atrosanguineus **71**, 146, 149, 150, 152
Cota austriaca **20**, 145, 146, 148, 150, 166, 167
cotton lavender 111
cowslip 13, **78**
Crataegus monogyna **128**, 144, 145, 167
Crocus chrysanthus 167
crown imperial 30, **31**
Cupressaceae 124, 137
curry plant 59
cut-leaf lilac 113
Cytisus 'Porlock' **93**, 144, 145, 147, 162

D
daffodil
 paper-white 10
 pheasant's eye **36**
Damask rose 108
Daphne
 bholua 94, 142, 143, 160, 167
 'Alba' 94
 'Jacqueline Postill' **94**
 var. *glacialis* 'Gurkha' 94
 laureola 94, 142, 143, **157**, 167
 subsp. *philippi* 94
 mezereum **95**, 142, 143, 156
 f. *alba* 95
 odora
 'Aureomarginata' **95**, 142, 143, 160
 'Rogbret' 95
Deutzia 104
Dianthus
 barbatus 20, **72**, 146, 148, 149, 150, 152, 156, 158, 159, 160, 164
 caryophyllus **72**, 146, 148, 149, 150, 152, 156, 158, 159, 160, 164
dill **12**, 57

Dipelta floribunda 96, 144, 145, 147, 160
Disporopsis pernyi **72**, 144, 146, 149, 167
Drimys winteri **128**, 142, 143, 144

E
early flowering hybrid lilac 117
Edgeworthia chrysantha **96**, 142, 143, 144, 162
　'Grandiflora' 96
　'Red Dragon' 96, **146**, 156, 157
edible fig **98**
Ehretia
　acuminata 129
　dicksonii 129, 145, 147
Elaeagnaceae 96, 97
Elaeagnus
　macrophylla 96
　pungens 96
　umbellata 97, 144, 145, **161**, 167
　× *ebbingei* 96
　× *submacrophylla* 96, **97**, 154, 161, 167
Emmenopterys henryi 129
English lavender 101
English rose cultivars 15
Erica arborea **97**, 98, 142, 143, 144, 164, 167
　'Albert's Gold' 97
Ericaceae 97, 106, 121
Erysimum
　cheiri 20, 144, 145, 146, 156, 164
　'Rysi Copper' **20**, 158
　'Winter Passion' **146**, 157
escallonia 98
Escallonia illinita 7, **98**, 142, 143, 144, 164, 166
Escalloniaceae 98
Eucalyptus **130**, 142, 143, 144, 145, 146, 149, 166
　gunnii 130
　pauciflora subsp. *niphophila* 130
evening primrose 14, **25**
evening-scented primrose 16
evergreen clematis **43**
evergreen Solomon's seal **72**

F
Fabaceae 22, 45, 52, 53, 83, 92, 93, 112, 117, 124
fairy flower 33
Farrer viburnum **119**
feathered Persian lilac **113**
fennel 6, **59**
feverfew **65**

Ficus carica **98**, 166
fig 98
Filipendula ulmaria 72, **73**
Foeniculum vulgare **59**, 148, 150, 162, **166**
　'Giant Bronze' **59**
forsythia 82
　white 82
fountain butterfly bush **85**
four o'clock flower **24**
foxglove tree **134**
fragrant cloud Shizuka **136**
fragrant snowball **118**
fragrant virgin's bower **43**
freesia 29
Freesia refracta **29**, 144, 145, 161
French lavender **101**
French parsley **57**
French tarragon **58**
fringe tree **88**
Fritillaria imperialis **30**, **31**, 144, 145, 158

G
Galanthus elwesii 'S. Arnott' **30**, 142, 143, 164, 167
Galium odoratum **73**, 144, 145, 146, 149, 164, 166
Gallica rose **108**
Galtonia candicans 37
garden mint **62**
garden pinks **20**
garlic
　society **38**
　wild **28**
Genista 'Porlock' **93**
Geraniaceae 74
Geranium macrorrhizum **74**, 145, 146, 149, 150, 152, 160, 166, 167
　'Ingwersen's Variety' 74
　'White Ness' 74
giant Himalayan lily **28**
ginger 8
Gladiolus murielae **32**, 150, 152, 154, 164
glaucous scorpion-vetch **92**
glossy abelia **82**
golden buttons **65**
golden currant **107**
golden-edged daphne **95**
gorse 14
　common **117**
Grossulariaceae 107
gum rockrose **89**
gum trees **130**

H
Hamamelidaceae 93, 99
Hamamelis 93
　mollis **99**
　vernalis 99
　× *intermedia* **99**, 142, 143, 155, 162, 167
　　'Angelly' **99**
　　'Jelena' 99, **142**
harlequin glorybower **91**
hawthorn **128**
Helichrysum italicum **59**, 146, 148, 150, 152, 162, 166
heliotrope 16, 21
　winter **77**
Heliotropium arborescens 16, 21, 146, 148, 150, 152, 154, 157, 167
Hemerocallis lilioasphodelus **32**, 145, 146, 162
Henry's emmenopterys **129**
Henry's lime **138**
Heptacodium miconioides **99**, 150, 152, 166
Hesperis matronalis **74**, 145, 146, 149, 167, 168
Himalayan clematis **44**
hoary stock **75**
Hoheria glabrata **100**, 149, 150, 164
Holboellia latifolia **50**
holly-leaf sweetspire **100**
honesty
　annual **74**, **75**
　perennial **75**
honeycups **121**
honeysuckle 16
　common **47**
　Japanese 46, **47**
　winter **102**
hop tree **137**
hops **60**
Humulus lupulus **60**, 148, 150, 152
　'Aureus' **60**
hyacinth
　common **33**
　summer **37**
Hyacinthoides non-scripta **33**, 144, 145, **147**, 157, 167
Hyacinthus
　candicans 37
　orientalis **33**, 143, 144
Hydrangeaceae 104
hyssop 13, **60**
Hyssopus officinalis **60**, 148, 150, 152, 157, 166, 167
　f. *albus* 60

I

incense cedar 124
Ipomoea alba **21**, 146, 148, 150, 152, 164
Ipomoea purpurea 21
Iridaceae 29, 32
Itea ilicifolia **100**, 149, 150, 157
Itea virginica 100, 145, 147, 149
   'Henry's Garnet' 100
Iteaceae 100

J

Japanese clethra **91**
Japanese honeysuckle 46, 47
Japanese wisteria 52
jasmine
   Asiatic **51**
   Chilean **47**
   common **46**
   star **51**
jasmine tobacco 25
Jasminum officinale **46**, 146, 148, 150, 164
   'Aureum' 46
   'Devon Cream' **46**, **161**

K

Katsura tree 8, **125**
Korean lilac 113
Korean spice viburnum **119**

L

lady's nightcap 33
Lamiaceae 60, 62, 63, 64, 65, 66, 71, 76, 90, 101, 120
Lardizabalaceae 42, 50
Lathyrus odoratus 22, 146, 148, 150, 152, 158, 162
   'Almost black' 22, **23**
   'Cedric Morris' 22
   'Chrissie' 22, **23**, **159**
   'King Edward VII' 22
   'Little Red Riding Hood' 22, **23**
   'Primrose' 22
   'Valentine' 22
Lauraceae 61
laurel
   cherry **105**
   Portuguese **105**
   spurge **94**
Laurus nobilis **61**, 145, 146, 166, 167
Laurustinus 'Lucidum' 119
lavandin 101
Lavandula **101**, **151**, 167
   angustifolia 101, 147, 149, 150, 152, 158, 166
     'Hidcote' 101
     'Loddon Pink' 101
     'Munstead' 101
   latifolia 101
   stoechas 101, 147, 149, 150, 152, 158, 159, 160, 166
     'Kew Red' 101
     'Snowman' 101
     'Tiara' 101
   viridis **146**
   × *intermedia* 101, 147, 149, 150, 152, 158, 166
     'Edelweiss' 101
     'Grosso' 101
lavender 6–7, 13, **101**
   common 101
   cotton **111**
   English 101
   French 101
lemon 127
lemon balm 13, **62**
lemon basil 63
lemon thyme 13, **66**
lemon verbena **56**
lesser calamint **71**
lesser catmint 76
Levisticum officinale **61**, 146, 148, 150, 157, 166
Ligustrum
   lucidum **167**
   vulgare **102**, 147, 149, 150, 167
lilac
   common **114**, **116**
   cut-leaf 113
   early flowering hybrid 117
   feathered Persian **113**
   Korean 113
   Yunnan **114**
Liliaceae 28, 30, 33, 34, 39
Lilium
   candidum 33, 148, 150, 164
   martagon **34**, 146, 148, 150, 158
   regale **34**, 146, **148**, 164
lily
   giant Himalayan **28**
   Madonna 33
   Martagon **34**
   perfumed fairy lily **29**
   regal lily **34**
   Turk's cap 34
   yellow daylily **32**
lily of the valley **29**
lime basil 63
Lobularia maritima **24**, 146, 148, 150, 152, 167
   'Snowdrift' 24
Lonicera
   fragrantissima **102**, 142, 143, **155**, 164, 167
   japonica 46, 142, 143, 144, 162, 167
   periclymenum **10**, **47**, 148, 150, 152, 161, 167
     'Graham Thomas' 47
     'Rhubarb and Custard' 47
   standishii **102**
   × *purpusii* 'Winter Beauty' 102, 142, 143, 155, 164
lovage **61**
Lunaria
   annua 74
   rediviva **75**, 145, 146, 149, 150, 167

M

Madonna lily 33
Magnolia 131
   doltsopa **131**, 143, 144, 145
   figo **131**, 132, 144, 145, 147, 162
   grandiflora **132**, 150, 152
   sieboldii **132**, 145, 147, 149
   stellata **133**, 143, 144, 145, 147, 149
   virginiana **133**, **148**, 161
magnolia 131
   banana magnolia 132
   Chinese magnolia 132
   star magnolia **133**
   sweet bay 133
Malvaceae 100, 138, 139
mandarin 127
Mandevilla laxa **47**, **152**
marjoram 13, 14, 64
   wild 64
Martagon lily **34**
Matricaria chamomilla **62**, 146, 148, 150, 164, 166, 167
Matthiola
   incana **75**, 147, 149, 150, 156, 157, 160, 161, 164, 167
   longipetala **24**, 145, 146, 148, 159, 161
May bells 29
May tree 128
meadowsweet 14, 72
Mediterranean sweet orange 127

Melissa officinalis **62**, 146, 148, 150, 164, 166, 167
Mentha
   arvensis 'Banana' 62
   spicata 62
   × *piperita* **62**, 146, 148, 150, 158, 166
      f. *citrata* 'Grapefruit' 62
      f. *citrata* 62
Mexican orange blossom 88
mezereon **95**
mignonette **25**
mints 13
   garden 62
   peppermint 62
   spearmint 62
   watermint 62
Mirabilis jalapa **24**, 146, 148, 150, 158, 160, **162**, 164
mock orange 104
Monarda didyma **63**, 146, 148, 150, 156, 166
moonflower **21**
Moraceae 98
morning glory 21
Moroccan broom **83**
mountain ribbonwood **100**
musk rose 7
Myrrhis odorata **75**, 145, 147, 149, 166, 167
Myrtaceae 102, 130
myrtle 102, **103**
Myrtus communis 102, **103**, **148**, 149, 150, 166, 167

N
narcissus
   bunch-flowered 36
   paper-white 35
Narcissus 35
   'Grand Soleil d'Or' **36**, 143, 144
   jonquilla **35**, 143, 144, 162, 167
   papyraceus 10, **35**, 142, 155, 164
   poeticus 35, **36**, 167
      var. *recurvus* 143, 144, 145, 164
   pseudonarcissus 36
   tazetta **36**, 143, 144, 145, 158, 167
      'Avalanche' 36
      'Martinette' 36
      'Minnow' 36
Nepalese paper plant **94**
Nepeta cataria **76**, 147, 149, 150, 152, 158, 166, 167
New Zealand cabbage palm **126**
Nicotiana alata **25**, 145, 146, 148, 150, 152, 154, 158, 159, 160, 162, 164
night-scented phlox **79**
night-scented stock 24
nodding virgin's bower 44
Nyctaginaceae 24

O
Ocimum basilicum **63**, 146, 148, 150, 166, 167
Oenothera biennis **25**, 146, 148, 150, 152, 162, 167
Oleaceae 46, 82, 88, 102, 103, 113, 114, 117, 126
oleaster **96**
olive
   autumn **97**
   sweet 103
Onagraceae 25
orange ball tree **86**
oregano 64
oriental poppy 14
Origanum
   majorana 64
   vulgare **64**, 148, 150, 152, 158, 160, 166, 167
Ornithogalum candicans **37**, 148, 150, 152, 164
Oshima cherry 136, **137**
Osmanthus
   decorus 103
   delavayi **17**, **103**, 143, 144, 167
   × *burkwoodii* **103**, 143, 144, **155**, 167
oxlips 7

P
Paeonia lactiflora **76**, 147, 149, 160
   'Dinner Plate' 76
   'Félix Crousse' 76
   'Sarah Bernhardt' 76
Paeoniaceae 76
palm
   Cornish palm 126
   New Zealand cabbage **126**
   Torbay 126
paperbush **96**
paper-white daffodil 10
paper-white narcissus 35
Parrotia **93**
parsley 13, 57
   French 57
Paulownia tomentosa **134**, 145, 147, 167
Paulowniaceae 134

peppermint **62**
perennial honesty **75**
perennial phlox **77**
perfumed fairy lily **29**
Persian silk tree **124**
Petasites
   fragrans **77**
   pyrenaicus **77**, 142, 143, 155, 159, 167
pheasant's eye daffodil **36**
Philadelphus **104**, 167
   'Belle Etoile' **149**, 164
   coronarius **104**, 147, 149, 164
      'Aureus' 104
      'Fragrant Falls' **104**, 107
      'Lemoinei' **104**, 147, 149, 164
   microphyllus **104**, 147, 149, 165
      'Virginal' **104**, 147, 149, 164
phlox
   night-scented **79**
   perennial **77**
Phlox
   divaricata **77**, 145, 147, 157
   paniculata **77**, 147, 149, 150, 152, 156, 158, 160
   'Fuji' **77**
pineapple broom 83
Polemoniaceae 77
Polygonatum odoratum **38**, 144, 145, 146, 157, 167
poppy 20
   oriental **14**
Portuguese laurel **105**
primrose **78**
   evening 14, **25**
   evening-scented 16
Primula
   veris **78**, 144, 145, 162, 167
   vulgaris **78**, 143, 144, 145, 162, 167
Primulaceae 78
privet **102**
Prunus
   laurocerasus **105**, 143, 144, 164, 167
   lusitanica **105**, 145, 147, 164
   'Otto Luykens' **105**
   serrulata
      'Jo-Nioi' **134**, **144**, 145, **164**, 167
      'Taki-Nioi' **136**, 144, 145, 167
      'Shizuka' **135**, 136, 144, 145, 167
   speciosa 136, **137**, 142, 143, 144, 167
Ptelea trifoliata **137**, 147, 149, 157, 166, 167
purple sage **166**

R

ransoms 28
Ranunculaceae 42, 43, 44, 45, 70
regal lily 34
Reseda odorata **25**, 146, 148, 150, 152, 154, 162
Resedaceae 25
Rhamnaceae 92
rhododendron **106**
Rhododendron
   fortunei 106
   griffithianum 106
   'Loderi King George' 106, **143**, 144, 164
   luteum **106**, 145, 147, 162
   occidentale 106
   viscosum 106
Ribes
   aureum var. *villosum* 107
   odoratum **107**, 143, 144, 162
Rosa
   'Charles Darwin' **109**, 147, 149, 150, 152, 162
   'Compassion' **48**, 146, 148, 150, 152, 154
   'Felicia' **109**, 147, 149, 150, 152, 160
   gallica 'Officinalis' 108
   'Generous Gardener' **49**, 146, **149**, 148, 150, 152, 160
   helenae **48**, 49, 146, 148, 164
   'Kew Rambler' **48**, 146, 148, **160**
   mundi 108
   'Paul's Himalayan Musk' **49**, 146, 148, 160
   'Rambling Rector' **49**, 146, 148, 164
   'Roseraie de l'Haÿ' **109**, 147, 149, 150, 152, 158
   roxburghii **110**, 145, 147, 160, 167
   rugosa **110**, 147, 149, 150, 160
   'Shropshire Lass' **49**, 146, 148, 150, 160
   × *alba* 'Alba Semiplena' **108**, 147, 149, 164
   × *centifolia* **108**, 147, **149**, 160
Rosaceae 72, 105, 110, 128, 134, 136
rose glory bower **90**
rose 7, 48, 108
   burr **110**
   cabbage **108**
   chestnut 110
   Damask rose 108
   eglantine 7
   English climbing **11**
   English cultivars 15
   Gallica rose 108
   musk 7
   rugosa **110**
   sweet chestnut 110
rosemary 6, **64**
Rosmarinus officinalis 64
rosy dipelta **96**
Rubiaceae 73, 129
rugosa rose **110**
Russian tarragon 58
Rutaceae 88, 112, 127, 137

S

sage 65
   common **65**
   purple **166**
Salicaceae 83, 84
Salvia
   officinalis 167
   rosmarinus **64**, 144, 145, 146, 148, 150, 152, 154, 155, 158, 166
      'Miss Jessopp's Upright' 64
      'Rosea' 64
   vulgaris **65**, 146, 148, 150, 158, 166, 167
Sambucus nigra **107**, 145, 147, 149
   'Black Lace' **107**
Santolina chamaecyparissus **111**, **146**, 147, 149, 150, 162, **163**, 166
   'Nana' 111
Sarcococca
   confusa **111**, 112, 142, 143, 155, 164, 167
   hookeriana var. *digyna* **111**, 142, 143, 154, 155, 164, 167
sausage vine **50**
saw-toothed azara **84**
scented jonquil **35**
scented mayweed **62**
scented Solomon's seal **38**
Scrophulariaceae 79, 85, 86
seven sons tree **99**
Shizuka cherry **135**, 136
silver lime **139**
skimmia **112**
Skimmia
   japonica
      'Fragrant Cloud' **112**, 144, 145, 164
      'Nymans' 112
   × *confusa*
      'Kew Green' **112**, 144, 145, 164
      'Kew White' 112
snail vine **45**
snowdrop 14, **30**
society garlic **38**
Solanaceae 25
Solomon's seal
   evergreen **72**
   scented **38**
South African sage wood **86**
Spanish bluebell **33**
Spanish broom **112**
Spanish traveller's joy **43**
Spartium junceum **5**, 112, **113**, 147, 149, 150, 152, 162
spearmint **62**
spurge laurel **94**
star jasmine **51**
star magnolia **133**
Stauntonia
   coriacea **50**, 144, 145, 161, 167
   latifolia **50**, 144, 145, 157, 167
stocks
   Brompton **75**
   hoary **75**
   night-scented **24**
summer hyacinth **37**
swamp azalea **106**
sweet Alison **24**
sweet alyssum **24**
sweet autumn clematis **44**
sweet basil **63**
sweet bay **61**
sweet bay magnolia **133**
sweet box **111**
sweet chestnut rose **110**
sweet cicely **75**
sweet Michelia **131**
sweet olive **103**
sweet pea **22**, **23**
sweet pepper bush **91**
sweet rocket **74**
sweet violet **79**
sweet William 20, **72**
   wild **77**
sweet woodruff **73**
sweet-scented columbine **70**
Syringa
   laciniata **113**, 144, 145, **159**
   meyeri **113**, 144, 145, 147, 159
      'Palibin' 113
   oblata **117**
   persica 113
   tomentella subsp. *yunnanensis* **114**, 145, 147, 149, 164
   vulgaris 114, 117, 144, 145, 147, 156, 158, 167
      'Anna Nickels' **114**

'Heavenly Blue' 114, **115**
'Joan Dunbar' 114, **115**
'Le Notre' 115, **116**, **144**
'Madame Antoine Buchner' 115, **116**
'Monument' 114, **115**, **164**
'Nadezhda' 114, **116**
'Sensation' 114, **115**, **176**
× *hyacinthiflora* 117, 144, 145, 156, 158
　'Esther Staley' **117**
　'The Bride' **117**
　'Turgot' **117**
× *Persica* var. *laciniata* 113

T
Tanacetum
　parthenium **65**, 146, 148, 150, 152, 158, 164, 166
　vulgare 65, **66**, 146, 148, 150, 162, 166, 167
tansy 13, 65, 66
tarragon 57, 58
　French 58
　Russian 58
three-flowered zabelia **120**
Thuja plicata 137, **138**
thyme 6, 7, 66, **67**
　common 66, **67**
　lemon **13**, 66
Thymelaeaceae 94, 95, 96
Thymus
　pulegioides 66
　vulgaris 66, **67**, 145, 146, 148, 160, 166, 167
　× *citriodorus* 66, 146, 148, 150, 158, 166, 167
Tilia
　henryana **138**, 150, **153**, 161, 167
　tomentosa **139**, 147, 149, 161, 167
tobacco plant 16
Torbay palm 126
Trachelospermum
　asiaticum **51**, 146, 148, 150, 161
　　'Pink Showers' 51
　jasminoides 51, 146, **147**, 148, 150, 164
　　'Variegatum' **52**
tree heather 97
Tulbaghia violacea **38**, **158**
Tulipa
　'Angélique' 39
　'Ballerina' 39
　'Bellona' 39
　Darwin hybrids 39

'Ad Rem' 39
'Apeldoorn' 39
'Golden Apeldoorn' 39
hybrids **39**, 144, 145, 156, 157, 158, 159, 160, 161, 162, 164
'Monte Carlo' 39
'Orange Princess' 39
'Princess Irene' 39
sylvestris **39**, 143, 144, 162
'Verona' 39
Turk's cap lily 34

U
Ulex europaeus **117**, 142, 143, 144, 145, 162, 167
　'Flore Pleno' 117

V
Verbenaceae 56
Viburnaceae 107, 118
viburnum
　bodnant 118
　Farrer 119
　Korean spice 119
Viburnum
　carlesii 118, **119**, **143**, 144, 145, 167
　　'Aurora' 119
　farreri 118, **119**, 142, 143, **154**, 155, 164, 167
　grandiflorum 118
　macrocephalum 118
　tinus 119
　　'Lucidum' **119**, 142, 143, 155, 164
　× *bodnantense* **118**, 142, 143, 144, 145, 160, 167
　　'Charles Lamont' 118
　　'Dawn' 8, 118
　　'Deben' 118
　× *carlcephalum* **118**, 143, 144. 145, 164, 167
Vigna caracalla 45
Viola odorata **79**, 142, 143, 144, 157, 167
Violaceae 79
violet 7, 13
　sweet **79**
Virginian sweet spire 100
Vitex agnus-castus **120**, 150, 152, 154, 159, 166

W
wallflowers 20, 21
watermint 62
western azalea 106

western red cedar 137, **138**
white forsythia 82
white-flowered borage 12
wild garlic **28**
wild marjoram 64
wild sweet William 77
wild tulip **39**
willows 14
winter hazel **93**
winter heliotrope 77
winter honeysuckle **102**
winter sweet **87**
winter's bark **128**
Winteraceae 128
wisteria
　Chinese **53**
　Japanese 52
Wisteria
　floribunda **52**, 145, 146, 157
　　'Alba' **52**
　sinensis **4**, **53**, 145, 146, 158, 159, 167
witches' thimbles 33
woodbine 7
wormwood 70

Y
yarrow **70**
yellow azalea 106
yellow catalpa **125**
yellow daylily **32**
Yucca filamentosa **121**
　'Bright Edge' 121
Yunnan lilac **114**

Z
Zabelia triflora **120**, 147, 149, 164
Zaluzianskya ovata **79**, 147, 149, 150, 152, 164
Zenobia pulverulenta **121**, 147, 149, 164

OVERLEAF
Syringa 'Sensation'